STRATEGY
Power Plays

How the World's Most

Strategic Minds

Reach the Top of Their Game

McGraw–Hill

New York · Chicago · San Francisco
Lisbon · London · Madrid · Mexico City · Milan
New Delhi · San Juan · Seoul · Singapore
Sydney · Toronto

The *McGraw·Hill* Companies

1 2 3 4 5 6 7 8 9 0 DOC/DOC 0 9 8 7 6

ISBN-13: 978-0-07-147560-0
ISBN-10: 0-07-147560-5

McGraw-Hill books are available at special quantity discounts to use as premiums and sales promotions, or for use in corporate training programs. For more information, please write to the Director of Special Sales, Professional Publishing, McGraw-Hill, Two Penn Plaza, New York, NY 10121-2298. Or contact your local bookstore.

This book is printed on acid-free paper.

CONTENTS

INTRODUCTION

From conversations that we have every day with serious businesspeople like you, we know that you have an enormous need for news, information, and insight that is accurate, reliable, and unbiased enough for you to act on it. That is what *BusinessWeek* is known for, and what we are always striving to do better.

Our *BusinessWeek* Power Plays series takes this to the next level. In collaboration with McGraw-Hill Professional books, we have drawn from the best in the business—the world's leading managers, strategists, and marketers—to analyze how you can use the best practices and best ideas of these insiders in your own personal playbook. Each chapter is drawn from a *BusinessWeek* case study and is supplemented with a lesson plan to articulate the key learnings in that case study, "power moves" (practical tactics that you can adapt to your own situations), and "Monday Morning" strategies to help you stay focused on success and put best practices into action. In addition a downloadable slide show and other online features that will enable you to share these lessons with colleagues and team members, as well as to brainstorm new ideas and strategies, will be available to readers from BusinessWeek.com.

Jeff Bezos's strategy for transforming Internet retailer Amazon into a platform for global e-commerce uses its industry-leading Web features and technology. John Chambers turned former high-flyer Cisco Systems around by dismantling its cowboy culture. Fresh insights into how Michael Dell runs his business should awaken anxieties among CEOs who are targets of his expansion drive. At IBM, Sam Palmisano's strategy to turn IBM from a tech services company into a makeover artist for corporations would change the way companies conceive and manage themselves. Samsung's contrarian—and winning—business model favors hardware and gadgets over software and content. UPS is attempting to reinvent itself into a logistics resource for industries of all types. Consolidation is giving U.S. steelmakers the heft to compete globally, a revival told through Thomas J. Usher of U.S. Steel. Michelin's transformation is told through scion Edouard Michelin, who shook things up at a very traditional company before his tragic death in May 2006. Publisher Arthur Sulzberger Jr. of the *New York Times* has an ambitious strategy to overcome weaker earnings, a scandal's aftermath, and a changing media world. The France family, patriarch Bill, son Brian, and daughter Lesa, runs the lucrative NASCAR stock car franchise amid rising complaints that it is dominating the sport. And American Express CEO Ken Chenault, backed by an antitrust ruling, has a bold strategy to take on Visa and MasterCard.

One note about these case studies: they are drawn from up-to-the-minute *BusinessWeek* reporting and are therefore "snapshots in time." Every effort has been made to provide factual updates, but because of the nature of news reporting, some of the characters and circumstances that the stories are based upon have changed since the articles were originally written. However, we believe that the power plays in each case do stand the test of time and will provide valuable lessons, even in hindsight.

But the lessons from these leading companies and executives are just the building blocks for your own personal strategy power plays—ideas that you will be able to put into use on Monday morning.

*   *   *

Many people at BusinessWeek have contributed the ideas and case studies in this book, including Tom Lowry, Amy Barrett, Ronald Grover, Robert D. Hof, Peter Burrows, Andrew Park, Dean Foust, Roger O. Crockett, Spencer E. Ante, Cliff Edwards, Moon Ihlwan, Pete Engardio, Anthony Bianco, John Rossant, Lauren Gard, Michael Arndt, David Welch, David Kiley, Stanley Holmes, Christine Tierney, Ann Therese Palmer, Chester Dawson, Joann Muller, Mara Der Hovanesian and Diane Alford. Callista Chen provided invaluable editorial commentary. Frank Comes, Joyce Barnathan, Christine Summerson, and Bob Dowling developed the series with our colleagues at our sister company, McGraw-Hill Professional—Philip Ruppel, Lisa Lewin, Mary Glenn, Herb Schaffner, and Ed Chupak. Very special thanks go to Ruth Mannino for her excellent guidance on design and editorial production.

Stephen J. Adler
Editor-in-Chief
BusinessWeek

BRIAN ROBERTS: CAN COMCAST FLY?

Courtesy of Getty Images.

Streamline operations while merging the customer service competencies and cultures of two very different companies.

Prepare for growth by investing in technology that enables the delivery of value-added services.

LESSON PLAN

POWER PLAYER

Meet Brian Roberts, the Comcast CEO, whose influence in the media world is growing. Media companies tend to operate at the extremes: either they are unstoppable, or they crash and burn spectacularly. Roberts, CEO of the newly formed AT&T Comcast, is about to find out whether his media giant can fly.

This 2002 cover story by Tom Lowry, with Amy Barrett and Ronald Grover analyzes the issues facing Comcast CEO Brian Roberts.

MERGING TWO GIANT CULTURES

You would never know that Brian L. Roberts was about to be catapulted into the media elite. In mid-November, his company, cable operator Comcast Corp., is expected to close its $54 billion acquisition of AT&T Broadband, the biggest deal in the industry since the AOL Time Warner merger in 2001. But on this evening in early October, Roberts, all 6 feet, 2 inches of him, is in a decidedly unglamorous position: he's scrunched into the back of a Ford Econoline van, barreling back to Philadelphia after a long day of volunteer work on behalf of his company. The 43-year-old executive, in jeans and a black Comcast T-shirt a size too large, is literally on the edge of his seat as his teenage daughter dozes beside him. Several executives are nodding off as well. But Roberts is a live wire as he recounts his decision to bid for AT&T's huge cable business. "You only get one chance to redefine your company, and this was ours," he says.

A TOUGH NEGOTIATOR

Roberts practically grew up in the cable business (his father, Ralph, founded Comcast in 1963), and he has a reputation as one of the best operators and toughest negotiators around, but he has never faced a challenge like this. In fact, no one in the industry has. Roberts's new company, AT&T Comcast Corp., will be unprecedented in size and influence. Before the merger, he could count a respectable 8.5 million customers in four major cities. Now, 21 million customers in 17 of the top 20 cities will be hooked up to his systems. That's nearly twice as many as the next biggest operator, Time Warner Cable. Put another way, it's in one of every five homes in America that has a television. AT&T Comcast could bring in some $24 billion in 2003, more than Time Warner and Charter Communications combined.

Indeed, everything is increasing exponentially for Roberts. The company will have to handle nearly four times as many customer-service calls this year as Comcast did last year. The number of people working for him will just about triple, to more than 55,000. AT&T Comcast's debt will be a nation-size $30 billion. And this is an executive who does not like to travel so far that he can't return home at night to see his kids. Up until two years ago, he still held Comcast's annual meeting in the lunchroom.

Even more daunting for Roberts is the fact that AT&T Comcast will be so big that it is certain to shift the dynamic of power in the media business. Roberts, who likes to say that his favorite TV show is the midnight special on his own QVC shopping channel, will effectively be the nation's top entertainment gatekeeper. Think about it: nobody will have more control over which TV channels, Internet services, and movies are piped into U.S. homes—not News Corp.'s Rupert Murdoch, not Sumner Redstone at Viacom Inc.

SEEKING THE MASS AUDIENCE

Right from the start, Roberts will have the clout to do what cable executives have wanted to do for years: dictate what shows will reach a mass audience, and at what price. One crucial issue for cable operators, for example, is the cost of programming, their single largest expense. For years, content-driven companies such as Walt Disney, News Corp., and Viacom have had the upper hand. That's about to change. With his vast system, Roberts can now hold out for better terms, and other cable operators will ultimately benefit, too. Consumer advocates, though, worry about how thoroughly Roberts will dominate the industry. "AT&T Comcast will be the single most powerful media company in the United States," says Jeffrey Chester, executive director of the Center for Digital Democracy, a public-interest group that is a staunch critic of the Comcast-AT&T deal. "They will most certainly determine everyone's digital destiny."

The lanky Philadelphia native may not have been plotting to control cable, but he has methodically assembled the pieces of what could one day be a full-fledged media enterprise. He now has the cable subscribers. And, to many people's surprise, he could be on his way to getting a critical mass of broadband users—Taking AT&T and Comcast together, a total of 342,000 new subscribers signed up in the third quarter. Over the years, Roberts has accumulated a modest programming collection, too. He has bought big stakes in several cable channels, including QVC Inc. and E! Entertainment Television, as well as two Philadelphia sports teams (not for vanity, either—the unassuming Roberts has met the 76ers All-Star point guard Allen Iverson only twice in six years).

Still, Roberts doesn't talk about transforming the industry; he won't even use the words *synergy* and *convergence*. He's not much of a visionary, and he isn't even sure that he needs to get mixed up in

Don't let Roberts's modesty fool you. Even if its cable channel and sports team holdings are tiny in comparison to the empires of Disney and Viacom, Comcast is leading the way. Certainly, additional vertical integration could enable other distributors, such as satellite companies or radio stations, to reduce programming costs. Though it seems simple, few companies will ever have the chops to succeed at both production and distribution. Comcast is already one of them.

programming, a business that has brought grief to so many. "We don't have a clearly defined content strategy at this time," he says. His most cosmic pronouncement comes out like this: "We will go from a regional cable company to being a premiere provider of entertainment and communications services into people's homes."

SMALL STEPS TOWARD BIG TRANSFORMATIONS

Translated, that means that AT&T Comcast could be the first company to make good on the long-awaited promise of broadband. Consumers are just beginning to experience the benefits—and, for now, are willing to pay the costs—of faster and continuous connections to the Internet. With 21 million potential customers, AT&T Comcast will have the scale to actually make money selling all the services that can go with it, from streaming video to music to video games. If broadband still proves elusive, though, the company's prospects could be jeopardized.

Even if Roberts gets broadband right, he couldn't have picked a worse time to burst onto the scene. Media and cable companies have crumbled all around him. Investigations into the accounting practices at several cable outfits have cast suspicion on the entire industry. Questions about the quality of earnings persist. And the fact that companies have spent tens of billions of dollars to upgrade their systems and have relatively little to show for it after nearly a decade raises fears among some that cable might be the next telecom. Meanwhile, satellite services are proving to be formidable competitors to cable operators' de facto regional monopolies. Over the next five years, the number of satellite subscribers is expected to grow by 37 percent, to 26 million, while the number of households that receive cable, now 70 million, may not increase at all, according to PricewaterhouseCoopers. And the collapse in October of the proposed merger of satellite services DirecTV and the Dish Network seems to have only galvanized EchoStar Communications Corp. Chairman and CEO Charles W. Ergen to go after cable subscribers even more aggressively.

Any one of these problems would be worrisome enough. Together, they have led many investors to give up on the industry for now. Cable shares have lost 57 percent of their value in the past year, compared with a 15 percent decline for the Standard & Poor's 500-stock index. Comcast's shares alone have fallen nearly 34 percent, to about $25, since it reached an agreement with AT&T last December. "Investors want to see the proof in the pudding. Where's the cash? It's that simple," says industry analyst Alan Bezoza of CIBC World Markets.

Roberts has even more to prove. From the start, AT&T Comcast will be shouldering an enormous amount of debt in a weak economy. Roberts will need to reassure impatient investors that he can pare it down and get cash flowing again. At the same time, to keep disgruntled AT&T customers from defecting, he has to spend about $2 billion or so over the next two years to upgrade AT&T's poorly run cable systems, which turn in some of the lowest margins in the industry. There is also the tricky task of combining a regionalized cable company with a heavily centralized organization whose focus has been phone services. And Roberts will have to work with the man who initially and vehemently opposed the merger: former AT&T Chief Executive C. Michael Armstrong, 64, who will become nonexecutive chairman of AT&T Comcast, could be a disruptive force at a difficult time, pushing for phone services over cable lines even though cable operators don't make much money from that business right now. "I wonder if [the Robertses] realize yet what a hornets' nest they bought," asks a cable executive familiar with the AT&T system.

TRUSTED MENTORS

As Roberts takes control of the biggest cable empire ever, he will rely on the two people he trusts implicitly. The first is his 82-year-old father, Ralph. When they finally sealed the AT&T deal, after five long months of negotiations, Ralph walked his exhausted son to his room at the St. Regis Hotel in Manhattan. They had talked often about their dreams for the company, which Ralph had built up from a single system in Tupelo, Mississippi. On this night, Ralph whispered to Brian as he embraced him, "This is a miracle." Roberts's other confidant is Stephen B. Burke, 44, whom he hired away from Walt Disney Co. four and a half years ago to run the cable division. Burke and Roberts share an easy camaraderie. They talk by phone half a dozen times a day and still high-five each other whenever the merger comes up, which is often. These men have proven to be a capable triumvirate; together, they run one of the few cable companies that has generated positive cash flow.

But the financial, management, and strategic challenges that Roberts is now up against are immense. It's no surprise, of course, that his father thinks he will succeed: "It's not like AOL and Time Warner," says the elder Roberts. "We are in cable, and we bought cable." AOL Time Warner Vice Chairman Ted Turner, who has known Roberts for 20 years (Roberts sat on the board of Turner Broadcasting System Inc. from 1989 to 1996), thinks he will, too: "I'll bet my last dollar on Brian Roberts." As for Roberts himself, he says with typical understatement: "The first 24 months are all about execution."

He may be short on the vision thing, but Roberts has always had a head for figures. He used to drop in on his high school's financial advisor to chat, and he went on to study finance as an undergraduate at the University of Pennsylvania's Wharton School. For the next few years, he will be focused on just two numbers: $30 billion in debt and 21 million subscribers. Back last December, many believed that he had gotten carried away in the bidding war for AT&T Broadband. But Comcast's falling share price has had one benefit: because Roberts negotiated an all-stock deal, his effective cost per subscriber has dropped from about $4,500 to $2,400. Still, AT&T Comcast will start life with more debt than Time Warner and Charter combined. Although the company still maintains its investment-grade rating, $30 billion in debt doesn't sit easily with shareholders. "We're being tarred as a telecommunications company with a lot of debt and overhang from the deal," says Burke. "We are just going to keep our heads down and deliver."

FOCUS ON FINANCES

Almost from the moment he closed the deal, Roberts has been trying to figure out how to lessen his financial burden. He says he has a plan to decrease the debt by $5 billion in the first year; most of the money will come from a masterful arrangement that he recently struck with AOL Time Warner to unwind Time Warner Entertainment Co., a complex partnership between AT&T and AOL. Roberts seemed to get the better of the deal with CEO Richard D. Parsons, who's supposedly the smoothest negotiator in the industry but who was also desperate to settle the issue. AT&T Comcast will receive $2.1 billion in cash, $1.5 billion in AOL stock, and a 21 percent stake in Time Warner Cable—which could be spun off by mid-2003. Comcast's stake is valued at about $5 billion. The company will also sell stock in AT&T and Sprint PCS to raise cash. Lawrence J. Haverty Jr., senior vice president of State Street Research & Management, a Comcast shareholder, says that resolving the TWE matter "was absolutely terrific."

But Roberts is laboring under an entirely different set of expectations than he is used to. "There's a real show-me attitude now," he says. "Everything [the industry] says and does are dirty words." The fraud charges against the Rigas family, which ran Adelphia Communications Corp., and the Securities and Exchange Commission and Justice Dept. investigations at AOL Time Warner and Charter have made many deeply wary of cable companies. It doesn't help matters that no one in the industry reports real net earnings, that each company seems to have its own definition of capital spending, and that the companies can't even agree on what constitutes a subscriber. What's not to be suspicious about?

These scandals come at an unfortunate time for Roberts. And the charges of self-dealing against the Rigases must be galling to someone who prefers Amtrak to limos and buys sandwiches at the food court near his office. The outward resemblances to Adelphia are especially awkward; it is, after all, a family-run cable operator in Pennsylvania founded by a shrewd patriarch.

But the Robertses don't hide the fact that they still regard Comcast as very much their company. Even Brian's mother, Suzanne, an actress, has a weekly half-hour show about "living well" that airs on a Comcast channel. Brian pestered his father about joining the family business almost from the time he knew they had one. "When he was still in high school, I had him sit in the corner and watch me negotiate a loan with a banker. He was fascinated," says Ralph. Brian read *The Wall Street Journal* as a teenager, and even invested in the stock market (and this was the 1970s). After college, in 1981, he started out as a controller in Comcast's Trenton office. By the age of 30, he was the company's president. At a recent industry dinner honoring

Roberts, AOL Time Warner's Parsons said that his ascension to the head of Comcast was his birthright: "The crown prince has assumed the throne." Then he joked that the *mohel* at Roberts's *bris* had used cable splicers. Roberts could only reply: "Geez, Dick, nice."

SETTING HIGH STANDARDS

Now Roberts is trying to do what he can to set himself apart from his disgraced and disparaged colleagues. He worked closely with an industry task force that on October 21 released a voluntary set of guidelines on how to report subscribers and capital costs, a framework meant to give more clarity to Wall Street. Comcast has also recently disclosed more information about its accounting practices, for the first time breaking down how it capitalizes expenditures.

Like all cable operators, though, Comcast reports EBITDA (earnings before interest, taxes, depreciation, and amortization), a metric that some investors say masks whether a company has real net earnings. Cable executives always argue that the more important measure is free cash flow; if so, then AT&T Comcast should start to show positive results of the merger in 2004, when it is expected to swing from negative $300 million to positive $2 billion in free cash flow. That will rise to $5 billion in 2005, estimates Merrill Lynch & Co. Investors who are looking for real net earnings might be able to see those results as early as 2004, once the investments in upgrades begin to wane, predicts Goldman, Sachs & Co. analyst Richard Greenfield. Indeed, though many still believe that the entire industry is in trouble, over the next two years the leading operators could emerge from their spending sprees with better prospects. "You'll see more and more companies beginning to deliver on these long-promised services," says media analyst Tom Wolzien at Sanford C. Bernstein Co.

As Roberts begins to redefine the company his father founded, Ralph will not be too far away. They have always had a close partnership. Herbert Allen, the media power broker, once described it as "one of the most unusual relationships I've seen. I think they are equal in their respect for each other." At a time when some sons would be chafing under their father's watch, Brian still turns to Ralph for counsel. And at a time when some fathers would be heading for their vacation homes, Ralph will serve on AT&T Comcast's board and lead its executive committee. Ralph's and Brian's offices are next to each other, and the doors are always open. Brian can often be seen sitting across from his father's desk seeking advice. When asked why he didn't take off his jacket during a recent photo shoot, Brian said: "Oh, no. My father would have killed me."

Roberts hasn't had to hire many top executives—most have been at the company for years—but luring Burke away from Disney was a coup. Burke helped launch Disney's chain of stores and then fix the finances at the Paris theme park. Although Burke had no previous cable experience, he has quickly earned respect in the industry. "He's one of the best executives in media," says Jessica Reif Cohen of Merrill Lynch. Burke, who writes a dozen personal notes to rank-and-file workers each week, brings a certain polish and operational expertise to the company. As he says with the requisite modesty: "I take care of the plumbing here."

STRATEGIC HIRING

While Roberts is plenty collegial in the office, executives on the outside say that he is easily the most competitive man they know. Several years ago at Allen's media conference in Sun Valley, Idaho, Roberts was desperate to persuade Warren E. Buffett to buy Comcast stock, but not desperate enough to pull back and let the Oracle of Omaha play a better round of golf. (Roberts is still trying to persuade Buffett to buy.) But Roberts seems comfortable sharing power with Burke; no doubt their similar backgrounds make that easier. Brian grew up watching his father work hand in hand with Comcast cofounder Julian Brodsky, while Burke observed his father, Dan, president of the ABC Network, work closely with Capital Cities/ABC Chairman Tom Murphy.

Two years ago, Roberts saw the opportunity of a lifetime when AT&T announced that it would split itself in three. The phone giant's cable unit, AT&T

POWER MOVE

Many executives have slyly poached talent from their competitors, but few have been so clever as to swipe a star from a supplier. A move of this kind is especially ingenious in the cable industry, where each of the major players rules over what is effectively a regional monopoly. So while insider information from, say, Charter would be welcome, Burke's knowledge of the economics supporting a major content provider like Disney will go a long way toward making Comcast an unbeatable negotiator.

Broadband, had more than 13 million subscribers, several prized systems—and some of the worst numbers in the business. Its margins were as low as 18 percent in some cities, compared with industry averages of 35 percent or better. The systems had been neglected for years, first by ex-Tele-Communications Inc. Chairman John C. Malone and then by Armstrong at AT&T, who bought the systems from Malone in 1998 but stayed largely focused on telephony. While Comcast's systems are 95 percent upgraded, only 65 percent of AT&T's are. Since the deal was announced last December, AT&T has lost nearly 500,000 subscribers.

Burke says that his immediate goal is improving margins to at least Comcast's average of 40 percent within three years. He'll decentralize operations (AT&T customer service had been handled out of its Denver headquarters), cut costs (Comcast has already said that it will pare 1,700 of 4,000 jobs in Denver), improve customer service, and sell more premium-priced services such as digital cable or high-speed data. "What is good is that we've done this before with other systems we've acquired," says Burke.

Central to AT&T Comcast's success is the complicated business of broadband. "That's our critical product of the future because we can add on other services," says Burke. Analysts predict that about 30 percent of AT&T Comcast's subscribers, or 6.7 million homes, will be paying for high-speed data by the end of 2006. If they are right, that revenue will go a long way toward meeting Burke's goal of boosting AT&T's yearly cash flow per subscriber from $175 to a figure closer to Comcast's $300 level. These services are also key to fending off the threat from satellite, which can't offer such interactive products. Burke also is counting on selling more advertising; he believes that digital technology will make cable a more interesting proposition, since marketers will be able to target spots to individual subscribers or homes. Advertising revenue will be $1 billion next year, and Burke predicts that it will double in five years.

Although AT&T is a much larger system to swallow than any that Comcast has acquired in the past, few doubt that Roberts and Burke can manage the integration. But their talk about digital cable service, high-speed data, and video on demand as major sources of cash flow seems far too optimistic to many. Haven't cable executives been promising this for years? "I'd be shocked if you get 20 percent of homes on high-speed data," says Leo Hindery, an ex-president of AT&T Broadband and now CEO of the Yankees Entertainment & Sports Network LLC. Burke counters that Comcast now has an edge: a bonus from the TWE deal was a broadband-access pact with AOL. Although the terms have not been disclosed, the arrangement is said to stipulate that AOL will pay Comcast about $38 a month per new subscriber (consumers will pay about $55 for AOL and Comcast broadband services combined), at the same time delivering all those AOL customers to Comcast.

Roberts made it clear early on that most of AT&T Broadband's senior executives would be better off elsewhere, and many have already left. One person who is staying, though, may be the most difficult—the former boss. Armstrong has been criticized for his role in running AT&T; he was pushed to sell the broadband unit by his board of directors. At AT&T Comcast, he finds himself in the undefined position of nonexecutive chairman, surrounded by Comcast veterans. It sounds like trouble already. One Comcast executive says: "This was a face-saving situation, and Mike knows that." At worst, he could be a disruptive force; at best, a distraction.

So far, the Roberts-Armstrong relationship has been "constructively awkward," says one executive. Armstrong and Roberts have talked over the past months, mostly by phone, but he has not been part of Roberts's inner circle planning for the new company. Armstrong hasn't been included in strategy sessions or the weekend conference calls that Roberts holds from his home. Nor has he been invited on the road trips to inspect AT&T cable systems. Clashes are likely to arise over the telephony business: Roberts is uneasy about making a big push after so many others have tried and failed. "Mike is going to have to recognize this is a very different role for him," says AT&T Comcast director Felix Rohatyn, a former managing director at

POWER MOVE

In 2004, Comcast launched a hostile takeover bid for Disney, the legendary entertainment empire. Disney rejected the offer, and eventually Comcast withdrew. At the time, some analysts claimed that Comcast's reputation had been seriously damaged, while others applauded the company's investing discipline. Regardless, Roberts has proven many cynics wrong, as Comcast, despite its already enormous size, has continued to grow.

investment bank Lazard Frères. "He's going to have to accommodate himself to what Brian wants."

For his part, Armstrong says that he sees his role as helping Roberts strengthen the company's financial position. But given the opportunity, Armstrong quickly shows why he may be more of a nuisance for Roberts. He still criticizes Brian and Ralph for taking 33 percent voting control in the new company (they had 86 percent voting control in Comcast, through a special class of stock). Armstrong says he urged them to take 20 percent, particularly given the growing concerns about the concentration of power in the hands of a few shareholders. "This is a new company and an opportunity to do it right," he says. "If we paid a full and fair premium for the company, why should we give up control?" counters Roberts. "[Family control] has been good so far for shareholders," who have seen the stock split 12 times since 1971.

Roberts is as confident as the next CEO when it comes to his company's performance. But he's reluctant to talk about lofty goals. In fact, he says that he has pretty much junked the notion for now. As he puts it: "I don't get to relish this deal. I have to deliver." But his hesitancy to articulate what the company will look like in five years makes some people nervous. "Brian has to figure out, and fast, if he wants to be predominantly a distribution company or run a content company, enhanced by distribution, like supermen Rupert Murdoch and Mel Karmazin do," says Hindery. There is talk about Roberts buying Disney one day, though there's been no word from him. But who can blame Roberts for hanging back when so many media moguls with grand visions have been shown the door?

POWER MOVE

Comcast has continued to diversify its portfolio. Along with the three other major cable operators, Comcast formed a joint venture with wireless giant Sprint Nextel to provide the next generation of communication products and services, including the "Quadruple Play"—video, wireless voice and data, cable phone service, and high-speed Internet access. Convergence is now a reality, and another fierce competitor—the telecom industry—has arrived on the scene, offering video service to people's homes. The cable companies need to be careful. Otherwise, they could turn around and find that the telecoms have beaten them at their very own game.

Of course, right now Roberts simply doesn't have the money to do much of anything. A purchase the size of, say, a TV network is unaffordable; even something smaller would be unpalatable. Instead, Roberts will keep launching lower-profile cable channels, which he can count on breaking even almost immediately, given his 21 million subscribers. And he'll use his new influence to secure more favorable deals for the content he has to buy: Roberts expects to cut $500 million from programming costs. "No doubt there'll be new tensions in the relationships between distribution and programming companies," says AT&T Comcast board member Decker Anstrom, president of Landmark Communications Inc., which owns the Weather Channel.

These days, it's hard to say who has the toughest job in the business. But heading the country's largest cable company puts Roberts in the running, especially since he has placed the family business in a tough financial position at a time of skepticism about his industry. When Roberts said that he doesn't have time to savor the AT&T deal, he wasn't just being modest. It's a good thing he didn't get into this for the glamour.

THE PROBLEM
Managing an enormous acquisition without losing focus on existing customers and operations

THE SOLUTION
Use your newfound scale to streamline operations and build negotiating leverage.

SUSTAINING THE WIN
Continue investing in value-added services, especially those that are dependent on broadband, to keep consumers loyal.

JEFF BEZOS: REPROGRAMMING AMAZON

©Thomas Broening

Diversify your revenue stream by adding new businesses to your low-margin consumer products retailing line.

Develop a technology strategy that allows you to get closer to big clients and facilitate success for thousands of small customers.

POWER PLAYER

Amazon is fast morphing into a tech company. With Amazon's industry-leading Web features and technology, CEO Jeff Bezos has grand plans for the once-struggling online bookstore to become a platform for global e-commerce.

This seminal article from 2003 by Robert D. Hof presents a fresh and intriguing view of the Internet retailer.

CRUNCH TIME FOR RETAILERS

It's crunch time for retailers, and Amazon.com Inc. is no exception. At its nine massive distribution centers from Fernley, Nevada, to Bad Hersfeld, Germany, workers scurry around the clock to fill up to 1.7 million orders a day—picking and packing merchandise, routing it onto conveyors, and shipping the boxes to every corner of the world. Like any retail warehouse running its manpower and machinery at full holiday throttle, it's an impressive display. But it's utterly misleading. The kind of work that will truly determine Amazon's fate is happening in places like the tiny, darkened meeting room at its Seattle headquarters where, one recent afternoon, five intent faces gazed at a projection screen.

THE STRATEGY IS TECHNOLOGY

Jeffrey A. Wilke, a compact, intense senior vice president who runs Amazon's worldwide operations and customer service, and an engineering team were trying out a "beta" or test version of new software that they had written. When the buying automation program is ready for prime time in mid-2004, Amazon's merchandise buyers will be able to replace reams of spreadsheets with graphics-rich applications that crunch data for them, so that they can forecast product demand more quickly and accurately, find the best suppliers, and more. The effort is one of scores of technology projects under way at Amazon that ultimately may change the entire experience of shopping online—and Amazon itself.

Just as most folks have come to view Amazon as a retailer that happens to sell online, guess what? It's morphing into something new. In ways that few people realize, Amazon is becoming more of a technology company—as much Microsoft Corp. as Wal-Mart Stores Inc. "What gets us up in the morning and keeps us here late at night is technology," says founder and Chief Executive Officer Jeffrey P. Bezos. "From where we sit, advanced technology is everything."

No, Amazon isn't selling its own shrink-wrapped software or leaving the retail business behind. But developing technology is becoming at least as important as selling Harry Potter books or The Strokes CDs. Indeed, some analysts say it's possible that in a few years so many other retailers will be using Amazon's tech expertise to sell on its site that they could account for more than half the products sold on Amazon.com. Says Bezos: "Amazon Services could be our most important business."

Already, Amazon's technological efforts have helped it reduce costs and boost sales so much that revenues are expected to surge 32 percent this year, to $5.2 billion. As a result, by the time the glittering ball descends in Times Square on New Year's Eve, Amazon may well reach a milestone some thought it never could: its first full-year profit .No wonder its stock has rocketed 152 percent in 2004, to $49.34 a share.

But all that is just the start. Building on a raft of tech initiatives, from an ever-richer Web site to new search technology, Bezos aims to reprogram the company into something even more potent. The notion is to create a technology-driven nexus for e-commerce that's as pervasive and powerful as Microsoft's Windows operating software is in computing. That's right: Bezos hopes to create a Windows for e-commerce.

SELF-REINFORCING CYCLE

Far-fetched? Not necessarily. After all, the Amazon.com Web site is already an essentially giant application that people simply use over the Web rather than in their personal computers. And bit by bit, just as its Washington neighbor did two decades ago, Amazon is building what techies from Silicon Valley to Redmond call a platform: a stack of software on which thousands or millions of others can build businesses that in turn will bolster the platform in a self-reinforcing cycle.

Since last year, Amazon has been steadily turning innovations that it developed for its own retail site into services that are available online. Using these so-called Amazon Web services, reached via a browser, merchants who want to sell more can use its patented one-click purchasing system, for instance, or tap quickly into sales data for particular products. Even independent programmers are getting interested: in just 18 months,

POWER MOVE

Selling software can be much more profitable—and difficult—than selling other products. Up-front investment in development costs, however, can produce payback in the form of staggeringly simple distribution.

up to 35,000 programmers have downloaded software that enables them to pick and choose Amazon services and, much as they do with Windows, write new applications based on them.

CREATIVE SPARK

Such developments recall the creative spark that launched the PC industry and, more recently, put the Linux operating system on the map. One program makes it easy to list products for sale on Amazon. Another lets merchants check prices at Amazon instantly via a wireless Web device when they're looking at stock to buy. It's a volunteer army that costs Amazon almost nothing. "I see them not just as a place to sell things but as a provider of technology," says programmer Paul Bausch, author of *Amazon Hacks: 100 Industrial-Strength Tips & Tools*, a new book on how to use the technology behind Amazon's site.

Amazon doesn't make money directly from the Web services. Merchants and developers can get free access to the services and can use them to sell from any outpost on the Web. Still, many of the merchants who use applications spawned by Amazon's Web services end up selling their wares to the 37 million customers assembled at Amazon.com. When that happens, Amazon takes a commission of about 15 percent, and these revenues have much higher margins than Amazon's own retail business. Already, 22 percent of Amazon's unit sales are by other merchants—and the Web services push hasn't had a significant impact yet.

BUSTING OUT OF RETAIL

While Amazon isn't getting out of retailing, its tech initiatives could, to some extent, set it free. By beefing up its technology and distributing it more freely, Amazon could bust out of the conceptual prison of stores and the virtual confines of a single Web site. Says e-commerce consultant and author John Hagel III: "It's really breaking apart the whole store metaphor." Into what? Amazon has already applied its own technology to forge an identity as an online mall—a piece of business that generates gross margins

POWER MOVE

Unlike traditional software economic models (selling a license for a one-time fee), Amazon's commission system generates a profit on every transaction. And because it is free, piracy is not a problem: techie troublemakers have little to gain from replicating Amazon's free code.

about double its 25 percent retail margins. Plugging into its massive e-commerce system, thousands of retailers from mom-and-pop shops to Lands' End Inc. and Circuit City Stores Inc. sell through its site. Amazon even runs the Web sites and distribution for the likes of Target Corp. and Toys 'R' Us Inc., which are featured on Amazon.com.

If Bezos's new plans work, Amazon could become not just a Web site but a service that would allow anyone, anywhere, to find whatever they want to buy—and to sell whatever they want to sell almost as easily. For Amazon, that means that its finances could look considerably better than traditional retailers'. Already it turns over its inventory 19 times a year, nearly double Costco Wholesale Corp.'s 11 times and almost triple Wal-Mart's 7 times. Yet unlike most retailers, it hasn't had to trade asset efficiency for profits. Its 25 percent gross margin is nearly double Costco's and three points higher than Wal-Mart's.

How much Amazon can expand the narrow margins of retail remains to be seen. But if even the conservative forecasts of analysts are correct, Amazon has a lot of upside in coming years. Shawn Milne of SoundView Technology Group Inc. sees sales continuing to rise no less than 15 percent a year through 2008, to $11.3 billion, with operating margins steadily marching up from 7 percent this year to 11.6 percent in five years. That's hardly the territory of Microsoft, with its 35.5 percent margins, but it's more than double Wal-Mart's 5.3 percent. "You're going to see the company look a lot different from a retailer in terms of financial metrics," says Milne. "Opening up the technology to other sellers is what has gotten the Street interested."

BOTH RETAILER AND MALL OWNER

Bezos's vision won't be easy to fulfill. Trying to be a world-class retailer, a leading software developer, and a service provider simultaneously strikes some observers as a nearly impossible endeavor. Even some Amazon partners report shortcomings in merchandising and technical support. Others worry about Amazon's inherent conflict in playing both retailer and mall owner. "They're biting off a lot," says Forrester Research Inc. analyst Carrie A. Johnson. "That's their biggest risk."

Amazon is hardly alone in its ambitions, either. For example, eBay Inc., the Web's largest marketplace, is building its own e-commerce platform. Already, it boasts several million sellers, at least 37 million

POWER MOVE

Amazon's new business-to-business (B2B) component comes with several larger, more predictable revenue streams. Each large corporate account will be more efficient to manage than the thousands of individual accounts. Losing just one of these accounts could be fatal; however, if this initiative succeeds, sellers of all sizes will rely completely on Amazon's technology platform—and guarantee the company's success.

active buyers, and more than $20 billion in gross sales—quadruple Amazon's—and it is far more profitable because it doesn't handle goods. Increasingly, merchants of all stripes view the two companies as key channels to online customers. And eBay isn't the only contender. Search upstart Google Inc. and even Microsoft, each with its own Web services initiatives, also aim to be hubs for connecting both shoppers and merchants.

Still, Bezos's bet on technology has paid off so far. Consider what has happened in its much-criticized distribution centers, which Amazon spent $300 million to build. Back in 2000, they were eating up at least 15 percent of sales, partly because processes for picking and packing different items such as books, toys, and CD players weren't very efficient. Chutes holding pending orders got backed up when products didn't arrive on time. Rampant mistakes required expensive manual fixes. Software was primitive, too: workers had to enter data into the system using arcane Unix software commands.

A PAGE FROM DELL

Now, by most accounts, the warehouses hum more like Dell Inc.'s build-to-order factories. With a menu-driven software console, workers can anticipate where bottlenecks are likely to occur and move people around to avoid them. Another program rolled out this year sets priorities, based on current customer demand, for which products should be placed at the front of supply lines, further speeding the flow.

The result: Amazon's distribution centers can handle triple the volume of four years ago and cost half as much to operate relative to revenue, just 7 percent of sales. Wilke believes that further software improvements can boost productivity by up to 10 percent a year. "They couldn't do this without very, very good software," says

Stephen C. Graves, a professor of management science and engineering systems at Massachusetts Institute of Technology's Sloan School of Management who has helped analyze Amazon's distribution operations. Another bonus for Amazon: with fewer distribution mistakes, it has reduced customer service contacts per order by 50 percent since 1999.

All that has kicked off the virtuous cycle that's now propelling Amazon toward more consistent profits. Lower costs have enabled it to offer more product discounts and free shipping on most orders over $25. Those moves are credited with recharging sales—and with operating costs up only 5 percent this year, the benefits have dropped right to the bottom line.

Even so, Bezos isn't resting easy. While Amazon's spending on technology likely will remain fairly steady next year at about $216 million, thanks to declining tech prices, Chief Technology Officer Al Vermeulen says that he will hire hundreds more software engineers and computer scientists in the next year to slake Bezos's thirst for tech. "Jeff is a very big driver of the technology," says Amazon director Tom Alberg, managing director of Seattle-based Madrona Venture Group.

For one thing, Bezos believes that there's still plenty of room for improvement on the Web site itself. To that end, he hired last year what is probably a first for Corporate America: a chief algorithms officer, Udi Manber. His mission: to develop better versions of algorithms, the complex mathematical recipes that get software to do its magic. In particular, he's creating improved algorithms for Amazon's newest tech push: search. On October 2003 Amazon launched Search Inside the Book, a feature that allows visitors to find any word or phrase on 35 million pages in 120,000 books—and lets them read entire pages around those keywords. In the week following, average sales growth for those books was nine percentage points higher than for books that were not in that database.

Manber has bigger plans yet. He now heads Amazon's first Silicon Valley outpost, a subsidiary called A9 that's charged with coming up with cutting-edge search technology. It's not just a defensive shot at search phenom Google, which is testing a shopping search engine that it calls Froogle. "We need to help people get everything they need, not just a Web page," says Manber. And whatever he and his

Companies often dedicate resources specifically to innovation. Why? Truly creative thinking requires people to take risks, and sometimes to fail. In environments that don't punish failure, people are more likely to try new concepts or pursue seemingly crazy ideas—the ones that often result in the most revolutionary, exciting products and services.

team come up with—he's mum now—it won't be confined to Amazon.com. A9 plans to offer the search services it creates to other e-commerce sites as well.

CHALLENGES LEAD TO OPPORTUNITIES

Technologies like that, in which Amazon is reaching out beyond its own site, offer the most intriguing new opportunities—and challenges. Consider Amazon's Merchant.com business, which takes over the entire e-commerce operations of other retailers. By all appearances, it's a success. In Toys 'R' Us's most recent quarter, in which results were dismal, the one bright spot was a 15 percent jump in sales at Toyrus.com, run by Amazon. Other retailers seem happy, too. "Amazon is the most sophisticated technology provider and service partner on the Internet,'" says Target Vice Chairman Gerald L. Storch.

But how much that business will grow is debatable. As both retailer and mall operator, Amazon has divided loyalties. "Some companies worry about creating the next Wal-Mart that's going to take their business away down the road," says Dave Fry, CEO of Ann Arbor (Michigan)–based e-commerce consultant Fry Inc., which has helped several retailers sell on Amazon. As a result, many are going with rivals such as GSI Commerce Inc., which runs online operations for 51 retailers, from Linens 'n Things to The Sports Authority. Says Forrester's Johnson: "Ultimately, Amazon will be most successful selling their own and other retailers' products on their platform."

ALL ABOUT PLATFORM

That's why Web services, unfettered by logistical challenges or business model conflicts, may offer the most expansion potential of all Amazon's tech initiatives. Nowhere is the potential more apparent than among the small merchants and independent programmers who are flocking to Amazon Web Services. "It's like an ecosystem," says Bezos. "People are doing things that surprise us."

People like Cleveland Wilson, a former tech recruiter who started selling books on Amazon in early 2002. Until this year, he didn't even think his operation would bring in enough to pay his rent in Berkeley, California. But he discovered a program called ScoutPal that uses Amazon Web services to let booksellers type or scan a book's ISBN number into a laptop or wireless Web device and instantly see what it's selling for on Amazon. So when he visits thrift stores and garage sales, he can buy books that he knows will be profitable to resell. For example, he paid $8 for *Suicide and Attempted Suicide: Methods and Consequences* and sold it for $275. From $100,000 in sales this year, he expects to do $250,000 next year because he has cut the time it takes to buy and sell books by two-thirds. "Without Amazon Web services, I wouldn't be in this business," he says.

That's not all. Now, he's starting a company to develop his own software using Amazon Web services that will help other sellers improve their businesses. It's still early, but it's possible that Amazon has latched onto one of tech's juiciest dynamics: a self-reinforcing community of supporters. Indeed, it seems to be harnessing the same "viral" nature of the open-source movement that made Linux a contender to Windows. Says Whit Andrews, an analyst at Gartner Inc.: "It creates an enormous community of people interested in making Amazon a success."

Even Microsoft. In Office 2003, people can click on a word or name in any document and be whisked off to Amazon.com so that they can buy a related book or other product. Says Gytis Barzdukas, director of Microsoft's Office product management group: "It gives Amazon the ability to market to a whole new set of customers and to become a part of people's work processes."

Amazon, the next Microsoft? Not so fast. For all the promise, building a broad platform is about as tough as a goal gets in the tech business—as nearly every competitor to Microsoft can attest. And unlike most tech companies, Amazon has to contend not just with bits and bytes but also with the bricks and mortar of warehouses and the fickle fingers of Web shoppers. But for now, at least, Amazon's pursuit of cutting-edge technology has given it time to figure out what comes next.

MONDAY MORNING...

THE PROBLEM
Entering new, higher-margin software businesses
without losing focus on existing business units

THE SOLUTION
Invest up front in cutting-edge technology that will
secure distribution advantage.

SUSTAINING THE WIN
Form splinter groups to focus specifically on keeping
pace with innovative competitors.

JOHN CHAMBERS: CISCO'S COMEBACK

Great goals
many - SBUs
Change culture ✓

Courtesy of Getty Images.

POWER PLAYER

After CEO John Chambers belatedly hit the brakes on Cisco's operations, it seemed as if the company would never recover. After some rough waters, Chambers turned the company around, and as the economy heats up once again, Cisco Systems is ready to sail.

In this behind-the-scenes narrative from 2003. Peter Burrows captures how John Chambers managed the turnaround. .

LESSON PLAN

Reduce the size of an enormous workforce as respectfully and professionally as possible.

Instill structure in an acquisitive company without sacrificing its entrepreneurial spirit. Develop a framework to integrate all of your business units and divest the ones that don't fit.

Create a portfolio that includes both short-term wins and long-term growth prospects.

Use multiple incentives to help ease your team's transition to a new corporate culture.

FACE REALITY

For the first few weeks of 2001, John T. Chambers, the irrepressibly optimistic CEO of Cisco Systems Inc., thought the networking giant might neatly sidestep the tech wreck. Twice he had canvassed his top lieutenants, only to rebuff their advice that he lay off workers for the first time in the company's history. But on the evening of March 8, 2001, Chambers landed in Silicon Valley shaken by what he had learned during a two-week business trip around the world. Customer after customer had told him that they were slashing spending. Finally, he succumbed: it was time for a massive overhaul. He stayed up all night, hitting the treadmill for hours in his Los Altos Hills home. "I just ran and ran and ran, and thought through the alternatives," he says. At 4 a.m., he decided to call a meeting of his top managers for 6:30 that morning.

It was a gut-wrenching session. An unusually downbeat Chambers huddled with his top executives and then O.K.'d 8,500 layoffs—18 percent of the payroll. "This is the toughest decision I've ever had to make," he said, according to one person who was in the room. At 9:30, he left to break the news to employees at his monthly breakfast with workers celebrating birthdays that month. "He had serious feelings of remorse, of 'what could I have done differently?'" says Peter Solvik, the company's former chief information officer. "For a year after that, he was somber."

HOW TIMES HAVE CHANGED

How times have changed. When Cisco announced its quarterly results, Chambers was back to his ebullient self—at one point jokingly asking a vice president if he was sure he didn't want to raise his forecast in response to an analyst's question. His giddy mood spoke volumes, as did Cisco's results: the company's profits had zoomed 76 percent, to $1.1 billion for the quarter, while sales hit $5.1 billion, the highest level since January 2001. With orders on the upswing, Cisco said that it expects to post 9 to 11 percent growth in the current quarter.

Cisco isn't just back in fighting trim—it's stronger than ever. The company's share of the total $92 billion communications-equipment business has jumped to 16 percent from 10 percent in 2001, according to Synergy Research Group Inc.—the biggest land grab in Cisco's history. While battered rivals Lucent Technologies and Nortel

Networks are only now glimpsing black ink, Cisco is racking up record profits. It earned $3.6 billion in the most recent fiscal year, nearly a billion dollars more than its previous best in 2000. And with no long-term debt and $19.7 billion in cash and investments, Cisco's balance sheet is among the strongest in the tech industry. Says Chambers: "We've executed to the point that we have 100 percent of the industry's profits, 100 percent of the cash, and about 70 percent of the market cap."

REBUILT FOUNDATION

Indeed, Cisco could be a case study of how a sullied highflier can use a slump not only to clean house but also to build a better foundation. While Chambers was late to recognize the worst tech downturn in history, once he realized that it was no mere dip, he seized the moment to rethink every aspect of the company—upending its operations, its priorities, and even its culture. *Intro: Discipline*

Chambers replaced the chaos that went with growth at any cost with the order of a company managed for profits. Using a six-point plan, he imposed operating discipline on entrepreneurial staffers who had been too busy taking orders and cashing stock options to bother with efficiency, cost cutting, or teamwork. Engineers who had been able to chase any idea willy-nilly suddenly had to work only on technologies that had been approved by a newly appointed engineering czar. Midlevel managers who had had the authority to invest $10 million in a promising start-up saw the open checkbook snapped shut. Executives who had been encouraged to compete with one another found that teamwork would count for as much as 30 percent of their annual bonuses. And staffers who fueled Cisco's 73-company buying binge from 1993 to 2000 by scooping up any networking outfit with a shot at success were told that they would be held personally accountable for a deal's financial results. "Process was a dirty word at Cisco, including for the CEO," admits Chambers.

POWER MOVE

In this downturn environment, Cisco couldn't continue to swallow up companies without evaluating them more rigorously. And aligning executives' incentives with the company's interests in collaboration and accountability helped to accelerate the changes.

In all, it's the rare tale of an Internet star that turned out to be more, rather than less, than it seemed to be. It would be hard to overstate the battering that Chambers's reputation took in the first few months of 2001. He was relentlessly upbeat even as evidence of trouble mounted. Lucent, Gateway, and others announced layoffs, and still Chambers waxed optimistic. He didn't back off from projections of 50 percent revenue growth until February 6—and then only to 30 percent. He assured investors that Cisco's hyperefficient e-business systems enabled it to forecast demand with near-scientific precision. Then he was proven wildly wrong. After Cisco announced layoffs and a staggering $2.2 billion inventory writedown, Chambers looked like a corporate Goodtime Charlie, incapable of managing in turbulent times. But once his eyes were opened, he threw himself into the reality of a new, harsher environment with the same near-religious zeal he had given the Internet boom.

Cisco's conversion has been agonizing for many involved. More than 3,000 resellers and 800 suppliers were squeezed out as Cisco reduced its partnerships to cut costs. Some employees felt that the mass layoffs were a draconian overreaction. Even Chambers has paid a price. The 54-year-old West Virginian looks like he has aged ten years in the past three, with the lines around his eyes and mouth visibly deeper. "It was obviously the most challenging time in my business career," he says.

PINPOINT AREAS OF GROWTH

With the trying times behind him, Chambers now wants to put more distance between Cisco and its rivals. While he won't commit publicly to a specific growth target after being burned so badly, two high-ranking executives say that the internal goal is a scorching 20 percent a year. Is it possible? Cisco sees three engines of growth. For starters, the company already gets 14 percent of its sales from six fast-growing markets that it targeted during the downturn, including Wi-Fi and security software. It's also banking on an upgrade cycle in its primary business of selling routers and switches, the large computers that direct the flow of data on the Net and corporate networks. The third leg of Chambers's growth plan is grabbing a large share of the telecom-gear market as the world's phone companies go from running separate networks for voice, data, and video to a single, more cost-effective network to handle all three. Chambers thinks that

Cisco can boost its share of the $64 billion telecom market from 3 percent now to at least 15 percent, although he won't specify a time frame. Investors are optimistic: Cisco's shares have surged 80 percent over the past year, to 23.

Still, Chambers will have to struggle to live up to such sky-high goals. Investors and top executives may think of Cisco as a turbocharged growth company, but it simply isn't anymore. Even in the much-celebrated first fiscal quarter, Cisco's revenues rose only 5 percent. And that's not going to improve much in the years ahead. Why? It's the law of large numbers: the networking-equipment business, which accounts for 80 percent of Cisco's revenues, is expected to grow a piddling 6 percent in coming years, according to JMP Securities. Cisco will get a lift from expanding into new markets, particularly telecom, but it's unlikely that top-line growth will pass the low double digits for the foreseeable future. "I think they can get to 10 percent," says analyst Brantley Thompson of Goldman, Sachs & Co. "I don't think they can get to 15 percent. At some point, all the tech giants slow down."

POWER MOVE

At the time, wireless security and telecom networking were not large markets, and it will be years before technological advances will make them broadly appealing—and affordable—to the average consumer. Still, Cisco is smart to invest now, before its competitors do so.

CUSTOMERS CAN ALWAYS SHOP AROUND

Ironically, the going may get tougher as the economy rebounds. At the downturn's nadir, most corporations grudgingly paid Cisco's premium prices rather than incur the cost of switching to weaker rivals that might not survive for long. Now customers are starting to shop around—and there are bargains to be had. Dell and China's Huawei Technologies, in particular, are aggressively undercutting Cisco's prices. "Cisco is in denial," says Dell Inc. President Kevin B. Rollins. "In every tech market we've seen, prices and margins come down. It's a law of gravity." Also worrisome are the resellers and suppliers that Cisco squeezed during the slump. With the economy bouncing back, many bruised ex-partners, such as networking specialist Xtelesis Corp. in Burlingame, California, are eager to help rivals take Cisco down a notch. "They're not hurting now," says President Scott Strochak. "But once customers are investing again and Cisco has lost half of its smaller distributors, I'd like to think it will hurt them."

Cisco also must prove that its newfound discipline hasn't dampened its hard-charging zeal. Some recent departees say that there have been frustrations with all the new procedures, and they worry that bureaucracy may slow Cisco down as it battles nimble rivals. One sign of potential trouble is Cisco's inability to hold off upstart Juniper Networks in the market for the high-end routers that telephone companies use to handle massive data flows. While Juniper has been gaining share, insiders say that Cisco's years-long effort to field a competing product has been stymied by engineering delays. "Cisco has been too conservative," says Tom Nolle, president of consulting firm CIMI Corp.

Still, there's no doubt that Cisco's rebound positions it as a powerhouse for years. The company is more disciplined and cohesive, and Chambers's plans for new markets may change the very nature of Cisco. Besides security software and wireless gear, it's moving into storage-networking products, optical gear, and even consumer gadgets. Selling Wi-Fi gear is worth nearly $1 billion, and Cisco has begun rolling out consumer offerings, such as a $149 wireless security camera. All told, analysts expect the new businesses to account for 30 percent of Cisco's revenues in 2006.

DISCIPLINE PLUS ZEAL

The company's remarkable journey began as many difficult transitions do—reluctantly. In late 2000, contract manufacturers began warning that parts were piling up in their warehouses and asked for permission to cut back on orders. Cisco executives told them to keep ordering. Even after Cisco narrowly missed Wall Street's earnings expectations in the quarter that ended January 30, 2001—its first miss in 11 years—Chambers couldn't break from his growth-oriented mind-set. "John had always boldly gone where no one else would go," says Gary Daichendt, his former number two, who retired in December 2000.

All that changed during Chambers's around-the-world business trip in late February and early March. He realized that the world had changed—and that Cisco would have to adjust. "At times like those, you have to analyze what you did to yourself, vs. what the market did to you," says Chambers. "You almost always get surprised [by a downturn], but you determine how deep and long you think it will be, take appropriate actions, and start getting ready for the next upturn."

That process began at the meeting on the morning of the layoffs. From the start, the team agreed that the ultimate goal should be to maintain Cisco's net profit margin of 20 percent. They hammered out the details of the six-point plan that Chambers had begun sketching. Then they turned to the harsh task of determining how many jobs needed to go. Many were dismayed—even embarrassed—at having to issue so many pink slips just a month after they had hired 2,400 new workers. But Chambers wanted the layoffs to be large enough that he wouldn't have to issue wave after wave of cuts, as Hewlett-Packard, Sun Microsystems, and Siebel Systems had had to do. To ease the blow, Chambers insisted on rich severance packages and urged his team to be brutally frank about the deteriorating situation.

For weeks, Cisco's top 20 executives gathered daily in a conference room called Napa Valley, overlooking the green hills east of San Jose. One morning in April, then-CFO Larry R. Carter delivered more painful news: because Cisco had been buying parts like mad until demand fell off a cliff, it had mountains of inventory that was obsolete. He recommended moving quickly to take a roughly $2 billion write-off—20 percent of Cisco's accumulated profits since it was formed in 1984. Senior Vice President Randy Pond at one point offered to break the news to Cisco's board himself, since inventory was under his purview. Chambers cut him short. "Don't even go there," he said. "We got to this point based on decisions that were rational at the time." Still, even Chambers's reassuring tone couldn't soften the blow. "There were a lot of heads in hands," recalls Pond. When Cisco announced the $2.2 billion writedown on May 8, Cisco's battered stock slid 7 percent more, to 19.50.

It was during the summer of 2001 that Chambers and the rest of Cisco's management team began to control their own destiny. One of Chambers's first moves after the writedown was to visit Mario

POWER MOVE

Like American Express CEO Kenneth Chenault, Chambers believed strongly enough in his company not to cower when the economy slowed down. Instead, both executives used the opportunity to streamline operations and rationalize investments so that they would be poised to capture the growth that they saw around the corner.

Mazzola, a well-respected engineer who had joined Cisco in 1993. The Italian native, now 57, had long planned to retire—an internal memo about his departure had already circulated. But over several meetings at Cisco's sprawling collection of squat, three-story office buildings, Chambers told Mazzola that Cisco needed him.

The company's engineering efforts were a jumble of overlapping development projects. At one point, Cisco had five separate efforts aimed at data-storage switches, according to JMP analyst Sam Wilson. Chambers told Mazzola that only he could corral the company's 12,000 engineers and make Cisco a stronger innovator, less reliant on acquisitions. In August, Mazzola agreed.

STRICT DIET

He quickly got to work. Many iffy projects were axed, including a broadband wireless technology when the two biggest potential customers decided not to pursue it. In all, Cisco cut the number of models it sells from 33,000 to 24,000. Still, insiders say there's far more fat to cut. Says a former executive:"If you're 30 pounds overweight, you can lose 20 pounds just by walking—but [it takes more] to lose that last 10 pounds."

There's no question that Cisco has trimmed its once-freewheeling investment practices. In the past, acquisitions and investments in other companies were haphazard. That ended when Senior Vice President Daniel A. Scheinman took over corporate development in August. An attorney who had been Cisco's general counsel, Scheinman set up an investment review board that analyzes investment proposals before they can move forward. Roughly 50 percent are O.K.'d, he says.

The acquisition free-for-all ended, too. Scheinman set up monthly meetings with the heads of operations, sales, and finance to vet potential deals. Besides making sure that an acquisition makes sense for the company as a whole, the group works up detailed operational plans to make sure that the business can be successfully integrated into Cisco—and a deal's sponsor must commit to sales and earnings targets. That put a screeching stop to the buying binge: Cisco bought 2 companies in fiscal 2001, down from 24 the year before. The company is doing deals again, but more carefully. When Cisco bought home-networking leader Linksys Corp. in March for $500 million, Scheinman and his group talked for six months before proceeding.

Some of the most painful progress began during the fall of 2001 on the operations front. With Cisco's sales plunging, Pond's staffers began playing hardball with suppliers to keep profits up. The CEO of one supplier said that Cisco wanted to take 90 days to pay for his products instead of the normal 30. It also wanted the supplier to extend the warranty on its goods to three years from one. When he balked, the CEO got a call from a midlevel manager. "If you don't [agree to our terms], we'll instruct our people not to use your products," he recalls the manager saying. The supplier, like many others in such tough times, couldn't afford to lose Cisco's business and buckled under.

Many others lost out entirely. Cisco's list of key suppliers has fallen from 1,300 to 420. That lowered administrative costs and led to volume discounts worth hundreds of millions of dollars each year. Pond also outsourced more production to lower costs, going from 45 percent in 2000 to over 90 percent today. At the same time, he spent millions to shift production work from nine contract manufacturers to just four. And smaller resellers complain that Cisco began giving discounts to strategic distribution partners such as IBM and SBC Communications, leaving hundreds of smaller players unable to compete against these behemoths. "Cisco went from being our best partner in good times to our worst enemy in bad times," says the former CEO of one reseller. SBC says that the closer relationship is helping it sell more to its business customers.

In early 2002, with Cisco making progress in adopting Chambers's new marching orders, the CEO considered an even more ambitious goal: he approached CIO Solvik and asked him if it was possible to double productivity, to $1 million per employee, by 2007. That way, Chambers figured, Cisco could capitalize on the next spending upturn without having to add many workers, sending profits through the

POWER MOVE

When Terry Semel took over at Yahoo, Inc., he confronted the same dilemma that was now facing Chambers: how to stop being all things to all people. Like Semel, Chambers must develop a cohesive framework that integrates Cisco's disparate pieces—but doesn't narrow its scope too much.

roof. After a few months of studying industry leaders such as Wal-Mart Stores and Dell, Solvik said that it was doable—but only if Cisco stopped behaving like a confederation of start-ups and became more like a mature, cohesive corporation.

In Cisco's cowboy culture, this was explosive stuff. When Solvik explained his findings at Chambers's vacation home in Carmel, California, in April 2002, the response was chilly. Executives listened uneasily while gazing at the 180-degree view of Monterey Bay. When Solvik asked for volunteers to investigate how Cisco could emulate the best company in a certain area—say, Dell in operating efficiency—not a single executive followed through. "It didn't resonate well with the group at all," recalls Pond. "But Pete wouldn't let go of it."

Chambers backed Solvik. Just after the Carmel gathering, he instituted an Internet Capabilities Review. Three times a year, top managers share how they use the Web to boost productivity. At the same time, they're measured on how well they implemented the best ideas from previous sessions. He also created a series of committees to get all parts of the company working together. Now, most decisions—what parts to buy, what products to design, what distributors to use—must be cleared by Business Councils that focus on Cisco's overall performance.

All the new procedures created some controversy. Product managers were stunned at the extra steps required to get anything done. Under the new structure, Ish Limkakeng, a product-development manager for switches, must get clearance from a committee of executives from various parts of the company rather than just chat up a few associates. He says the change was difficult, although he came to understand the benefits for the company.

Some salespeople still feel hamstrung. One of Chambers's initiatives is an e-customer project that will consolidate 19 different databases into a single repository. It's designed to boost efficiency and prevent mishaps such as the double ordering by customers that contributed to the inventory writedown. But a salesperson can no longer log in an order for a new customer without first clearing it with a support team that makes sure that the customer isn't already in Cisco's records. One insider says that salespeople in Europe have been "thumbing their noses" at the e-customer rules and not following the new guidelines. Sales chief Richard J. Justice acknowledges some griping and says that Cisco may refine the process to address the complaints.

REIN IN THE CULTURE STRATEGICALLY

Chambers took other steps to rein in Cisco's Wild West culture during 2002. Most pointedly, he made teamwork a critical part of top executives' bonus plans. He told them that 30 percent of their bonuses for the 2003 fiscal year would depend on how well they collaborated with others. "It tends to formalize the discussion around how can I help you and how can you help me," says Sue Bostrom, head of Cisco's Internet consulting group.

When it came time to divvy up those bonuses, it was clear that Chambers's overhaul had resulted in a leaner, more efficient Cisco. On August 5, the company announced that it had earned $3.6 billion for the year—almost double its net income for the year before, even though sales were flat, at $18.9 billion. And employees were getting more comfortable with the new Cisco. "There's been huge progress," says Justice. "There's a sense of redemption and vindication."

Today, revenue growth remains the biggest challenge. The company is off to a fast start in a number of promising markets. In security software, Cisco already has taken the lead from Check Point Software Technologies Ltd., with a 27.3 percent share in the second quarter, up from 20.1 percent in 2001, says Synergy Research. And Cisco is building quickly on its Linksys acquisition. Charles H. Giancarlo, a senior vice president responsible for Linksys, says that Cisco plans to introduce a dozen more home gizmos over the next year. "Who knows?" he says. "Linksys might become a household name, while Cisco may only be for portfolio planners."

POWER MOVE

At the time, Giancarlo didn't realize quite how clear his crystal ball was. Today, the Linksys division is going gangbusters, preparing to fight the battle for the networked home. True, the fantasy—an affordable network of computers, electronics, and household appliances—may not exist for years. But Chambers knows, as he did with wireless security, that in time the technology will come, and the customers will follow.

Still, to get revenue growth back to double digits, Cisco will finally have to make headway with the big phone companies. And they're wary shoppers. Established carriers such as BellSouth Corp. had serious reliability problems with Cisco gear in the 1990s. To make matters worse, Chambers served as the arms merchant for scores of their upstart rivals—only to see most of them disappear in the telecom bust.

Now, Cisco has been on a crusade to get into the telecom industry's good graces. Chambers himself called top telecom executives to apologize for his past arrogance. "He said maybe they'd forgotten one of their fundamental rules: listen to your customer," recalls BellSouth Chief Technology Officer Bill Smith. Cisco also began pouring over 50 percent of its research and development budget into new gear that could be used more easily with the phone companies' existing switches. Cisco's most recent quarter suggests that the plan is going well: orders from carriers were up 20 percent over the previous year—far more than at rivals such as Lucent or Nortel. And phone company executives say that Cisco has made progress. "I think they are capable of becoming a top one or two provider," says SBC Chief Technology Officer Ross Ireland. BellSouth plans to deploy a Cisco switch next year to handle voice and data traffic.

After a difficult three years, much has changed at Cisco. At one point during the annual sales powwow at a San Francisco convention center in August, a wizened Chambers came out from behind the podium to be closer to the 10,000 salespeople. Dressed in casual clothes, Chambers squatted on the steps of the stage and struck an intimate tone. Recalls sales manager Gregory H. Lynch: "Chambers said, 'I think we're ready to grow again. I'm asking you to help me.'" The words are toned down from the wild years, but Cisco looks poised to continue its dominance.

MONDAY MORNING...

THE PROBLEM
Adapting an organization's aggressive growth strategy to a drastically slower market

THE SOLUTION
Instill discipline into every aspect of the business: strategy, systems, people, and culture.

SUSTAINING THE WIN
Stay true to your new business processes, even when business starts to pick up.

MICHAEL DELL:
THE SECRETS BEHIND
DELL'S EXPANSION

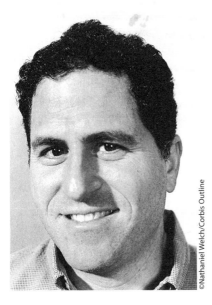

©Nathaniel Welch/Corbis Outline

POWER PLAYER

The founder and CEO of Dell Inc., Michael Dell, tweaks his management style to lead the company to even higher revenues and profits. How Michael Dell runs his business should awaken anxieties among CEOs who are targets of his expansion drive.

This November 2003 cover story by Andrew Park, with Peter Burrows, looks at the management secrets behind the best-run company in the technology industry.

LESSON PLAN

Enter new, highly competitive consumer-goods markets where you have little expertise and zero experience.

Use innovative organizational structures to ensure accountability and increase your impact.

Find new sources of revenue growth that make use of your core competencies.

Improve your leadership style without losing the competitive edge that has enabled you to succeed.

LISTEN TO FEEDBACK

When Dell CEO Michael S. Dell and President Kevin B. Rollins met privately in the fall of 2001, they felt confident that the company was recovering from the global crash in PC sales. Their own personal performance, however, was another matter. Internal interviews revealed that subordinates thought that Dell, 38, was impersonal and emotionally detached, while Rollins, 50, was seen as autocratic and antagonistic. Few employees felt strong loyalty to the company's leaders. Worse, the discontent was spreading: a survey taken over the summer, following the company's first-ever mass layoffs, found that half of Dell Inc.'s employees would leave if they got the chance.

What happened next says a lot about why Dell is the best-managed company in the technology industry. At other industry giants, the CEO and his chief sidekick might have shrugged off the criticism or let the issue slide. Not at Dell. Fearing an exodus of talent, the two executives focused on the gripes. Within a week, Dell faced his top 20 managers and offered a frank self-critique, acknowledging that he is hugely shy and that it sometimes made him seem aloof and unapproachable. He vowed to forge tighter bonds with his team. Some of the people in the room were shocked. They knew that personality tests given to key executives had repeatedly shown Dell to be an "off-the-charts introvert," and that such an admission from him had to have been painful. "It was powerful stuff," says Brian Wood, the head of public-sector sales for the Americas. "You could tell it wasn't easy for him."

Michael Dell didn't stop there. Days later, Dell and Rollins began showing a videotape of his talk to every manager in the company—several thousand people. Then they adopted desktop props to help them do what didn't come naturally. A plastic bulldozer cautioned Dell not to ram through ideas without including others, and a Curious George doll encouraged Rollins to listen to his team before making up his mind.

THE STATUS QUO IS NEVER GOOD ENOUGH

To some, the way Michael Dell handled sagging morale might seem like just another tale of feel-good management. But to those inside the company, it epitomizes how this Round Rock (Texas) computer maker has transformed itself from a no-name PC player into a powerhouse brand. Sure, Dell is the master at selling direct, bypassing middlemen to deliver PCs more cheaply than any of its rivals. And few would quarrel with the idea that it's a model of efficiency, with a far-flung supply chain knitted together so tightly that it's like one electric wire, humming 24/7. Yet all this has been true for more than a decade. And although the entire computer industry has tried to replicate Dell's tactics, none can hold a candle to the company's results. Today, Dell's stock is valued at a price-earnings multiple of 40, loftier than IBM, Microsoft, Wal-Mart Stores, or General Electric.

It turns out that it's how Michael Dell manages the company that has elevated it far above its sell-direct business model. What's Dell's secret? At its heart is his belief that the status quo is never good enough, even if it means painful changes for the man with his name on the door. When success is achieved, it's greeted with five seconds of praise followed by five hours of postmortem on what could have been done better. Says Michael Dell: "Celebrate for a nanosecond. Then move on." After the outfit opened its first Asian factory, in Malaysia, the CEO sent the manager heading the job one of his old running shoes to congratulate him. The message: this is only the first step in a marathon. *story - culture*

NO EXCUSES

Just as crucial is Michael Dell's belief that once a problem is uncovered, it should be dealt with quickly and directly, without excuses. "There's no 'The dog ate my homework' here," says Dell. No, indeedy. After Randall D. Groves, then head of the server business, delivered 16 percent higher sales last year, he was demoted. Never mind that none of Dell's rivals came close to that. It could have been better, say two former Dell executives. Groves referred calls to a Dell spokesman, who says that Groves's job change was part of a broader reorganization.

Above all, Michael Dell expects everyone to watch each dime—and turn it into at least a quarter. Unlike most technology bosses, Dell believes that every product should be profitable from Day One. To ensure that, he expects his managers to be walking databases, able to cough up information on everything from top-line growth to the average number of times a part has to be replaced in the first 30 days after a computer is sold.

But there's one number he cares about most: operating margin. To Dell, it's not enough to rack up profits or grow fast. Executives must do both to maximize long-term profitability. That means that products need to be priced low enough to induce shoppers to buy, but not so low that they reduce profits unnecessarily. When Dell's top managers in Europe lost out on profits in 1999 because they hadn't cut costs far enough, they were replaced. "There are some organizations where people think they're a hero if they invent a new thing," says Rollins. "Being a hero at Dell means saving money."

It's this combination—reaching for the heights of perfection while burrowing down into every last data point—that no rival has been able to imitate. "It's like watching Michael Jordan stuff the basketball," says Merrill Lynch & Co. technology strategist Steven Milunovich. "I see it. I understand it. But I can't do it."

How did this Mike come by his management philosophy? It started 19 years ago, when he was ditching classes to sell homemade PCs out of his University of Texas dorm room. Dell was the scrappy underdog, fighting for his company's life against the likes of IBM and Compaq Computer Corp. with a direct-sales model that people thought was plain nuts. Now, Michael Dell is worth $17 billion, while his 40,000-employee company is about to top $40 billion in sales. Yet he continues to manage Dell with the urgency and determination of a college kid with his back to the wall. "I still think of us as a challenger," he says. "I still think of us attacking."

POWER MOVE

Today, few people consider Dell an underdog. Although thrift still works, it can frustrate employees, who feel that the company is too large and profitable to be so miserly. It's so large, in fact, that like other erstwhile Davids— such as Internet ingenue Google, Inc.—Dell is being treated by consumers like the Goliath that it has become.

NO STARS

It's not that Michael Dell leads by force of personality. He's blessed with neither the tough-guy charisma of Jack Welch nor the folksy charm of the late Sam Walton. Once, after hearing about the exploits of flamboyant Oracle Corp. CEO Lawrence J. Ellison, he held up a piece of paper and deadpanned to an aide: "See this? It's vanilla and square, and so am I." This egoless demeanor permeates the company. Everyone is expected to sacrifice his or her own interests for the good of the business, and no one gets to be a star. If Michael Dell is willing to modify the personality traits he was born with, other top executives are expected to be just as self-sacrificing. Frequently, Dell pairs executives to run an important business, an approach called "two-in-a-box." That way, they work together, checking each other's weaknesses and sharing the blame when something goes wrong. One such executive calls Dell's senior leadership "the no-name management team."

All this has kept Dell on track as its rivals have gone off the rails. Since 2000, the company has been adding market share at a faster pace than at any time in its history—nearly three percentage points in 2002. A renewed effort to control costs sliced overhead expenses to just 9.6 percent of revenue in the most recent quarter and boosted productivity to nearly $1 million in revenue per employee. That's three times the revenue per employee at IBM and almost twice Hewlett-Packard Co.'s rate.

Still, for the restless Michael Dell, that's not nearly enough. He wants to make sure that the company he has spent half his life building can endure after he's gone. So he and Rollins have sketched out an ambitious financial target: $60 billion in revenues by 2006. That's twice what the company did in 2001 and enough to put it in a league with the largest, most powerful companies in the world. Getting there will require the same kind of success that the company achieved in PCs—but in altogether new markets. Already, Michael Dell is moving the company into printers, networking, handheld computers, and tech services. His latest foray: Dell is entering the cutthroat $95 billion consumer-electronics market with a portable digital-music player, an online music store, and a flat-panel television set slated to go on sale October 28.

Can Dell graduate from PC prodigy to corporate icon? Driving for nonstop growth will require grooming a new generation of leaders, which Rollins concedes is a major challenge given the company's pressure-cooker atmosphere. In the 1990s, when seasoned executives recruited from titans such as Intel and IBM quickly jumped ship, Dell learned that outsiders don't adapt easily to its demanding culture. And unlike in the past, Dell won't be able to count on stock options

Michael Dell wants to play his starring role—scrappy newcomer challenging industry titans—in another show. By essentially copying his own tricks (superior supply-chain management and extraordinarily efficient distribution), he plans to storm the consumer-electronics industry. It's a sure thing, as long as someone else doesn't copy him first.

to make up for the discomfort. Some 32 percent of its outstanding options are priced above the current share price of $35, and the company has sliced grants to about 40 million shares this year, one-third the 2001 level. Little wonder that so far, Dell has achieved only a modest improvement in morale, according to its internal surveys. "They need to work a lot on appreciating people," says Kate Ludeman, an executive coach who has worked with Dell since 1995.

"ONE-TRICK PONY"

Dell also faces an innovation dilemma. Its penny-pinching ways leave little room for investments in product development and future technologies, especially compared with its rivals. Even in the midst of the recession, IBM spent $4.75 billion, or 5.9 percent of its revenues, on research and development in 2002, while HP ponied up $3.3 billion, or 5.8 percent of revenues. And Dell? A paltry $455 million, or 1.3 percent. Rivals say that this handicaps Dell's ability to move much beyond PCs, particularly in such promising markets as digital imaging and utility computing. "Dell is a great company, but they are a one-trick pony," says HP CEO Carleton S. Fiorina. What's more, Dell has shown little patience with the costs of entering new markets, killing off products—like its high-end server—when they didn't produce quick profits, rather than staying committed to a long-term investment. "They're the best in the world at what they do," says IBM server chief William M. Zeitler. "The question is, will they be best at the Next Big Thing?"

For Michael Dell, inventing the Next Big Thing is not the goal. His mission is to build the Current Big Thing better than anyone else. He doesn't plan on becoming IBM or HP. Rather, he wants to focus on his strength as a superefficient manufacturer and distributor. That's why Dell continues to hone the efficiency of its operations. The company has won 550 business-process patents, for everything from a method of using wireless networks in factories to a configuration

Key competence: Process improve [handwritten]

of manufacturing stations that's four times as productive as a standard assembly line. "They're inventing business processes. It's an asset that Dell has that its competitors don't," says Erik Brynjolfsson, director of the Center for eBusiness at the Massachusetts Institute of Technology's Sloan School of Management.

Dell's expansion strategy is carefully calibrated to capitalize on that asset. The game plan is to move into commodity markets—with standardized technology that's widely available—where Dell can *unlike* [handwritten] apply its skills in discipline, speed, and efficiency. Then Dell can drop *HP* [handwritten] prices faster than any other company and prompt demand to soar. In markets that Dell thinks are becoming commoditized but still require R&D, the company is taking on partners to get in the door. In the printer market, for example, Dell is slapping its own brand on products from Lexmark International Inc. And in storage, Dell has paired up with EMC Corp. to sell co-branded storage machines. Dell plans to take over manufacturing in segments of those markets as they become commoditized. It recently took over low-end storage production from EMC, cutting its cost of goods 25 percent.

Dell's track record suggests that the CEO will meet his $60 billion revenue goal by 2006. Already, Dell has grabbed large chunks of the markets for inexpensive servers and data-storage gear. After just two quarters, its first handheld computer has captured 37 percent of the U.S. market for such devices. And Rollins says that initial sales of Dell printers are double the company's internal targets. With the potential growth in PCs and new markets, few analysts doubt that Dell can generate the 15 percent annual growth needed to reach the mark. The company has averaged better than 19 percent growth over the past four quarters, and on October 8 Rollins assured investors that everything was on track. "It's almost machine-like," says Goldman, Sachs & Co. analyst Laura Conigliaro. For the year, analysts expect Dell to boost revenues 16 percent, to $41 billion, and profits 24 percent, to $2.6 billion, according to a survey of Wall Street estimates by First Call.

What should help Dell as it plunges into so many new markets is the founder's levelheaded realism. A student of business history, he has paid close attention to how some of technology's legendary figures lost their way by refusing to admit mistakes. He cites Digital

Equipment Corp.'s Ken Olsen as one who stuck with his strategy until the market passed him by, and he hints that Sun Microsystems Inc.'s Scott G. McNealy could be next.

Dell, on the other hand, has reversed course so fast he's lucky he didn't get whiplash. In 2001, he scrapped a plan to enter the mobile-phone market six months after hiring a top executive from Motorola Inc. to head it up. He decided that the prospects weren't bright enough to offset the costs of entry. The next year, Dell wrote off its only major acquisition, a storage-technology company it bought in 1999 for $340 million. Dell backed out of the high-end storage business because it decided that the technology wasn't ready for market. "It's amazing how a guy who was so young when he founded the company could evolve as he has," says Edward J. Zander, former president of Sun Microsystems. "Guys that have been in the saddle for 15 and 20 years tend to get too religious. He's the exception to the rule."

POWER MOVE

Dell's ability to change direction is invaluable. Countless companies have thrown good money after bad, thanks to the all-too-human tendency toward nonrational escalation of commitment. Most often, this occurs when managers can't forget earlier investments— otherwise known as sunk costs.

Michael Dell, in fact, has one of the longest tenures of any founder who remains CEO. At 19 years and counting, he's second in the technology industry only to Oracle's Ellison. "This sounds strange coming from me," says William H. Gates III, who was CEO of Microsoft Corp. for 25 years before giving it up to become chairman and chief software architect, "but very few business leaders go from the early stage of extremely hands-on stuff to have a leadership style and management process that works for a company that's an absolutely huge and superimportant company."

One way Dell has done it is through his power-sharing arrangement with Rollins, à la his "two-in-a-box" philosophy. Brought on as a consultant in 1993 to help plot the company's first long-range plan, Rollins helped it recover from a series of miscues, including the bungled launch of its notebook business and a disastrous go at trading currencies. Three years later, Dell hired Rollins away from Bain & Co. to run North American sales.

Now, Rollins is the day-to-day general. He and Dell sit in adjoining offices separated only by a glass wall. During a pivotal meeting in the fall of 2001, Dell proposed that they agree not to make a major move without the other's approval. Working in tandem helps them avoid mistakes that the more entrepreneurial Dell or the more rigid Rollins might make alone. Says Dell: "This company is much stronger when the two of us are doing it together." And there's no question that Rollins is the successor. "If I get hit by a truck, he's the CEO. Everyone knows that."

THE GAUNTLET

Not that the current CEO is letting up. He maintains pinpoint control over the company's vast operations by constantly monitoring sales information, production data, and his competitors' activities. He keeps a BlackBerry strapped to his hip at all times. In the office, he reserves an hour each morning and one each afternoon to do nothing but read and respond to e-mail, according to one former executive. "Michael can be a visionary, and he can tell you how many units were shipped from Singapore yesterday," says General Electric Co. CEO Jeffrey R. Immelt, a top Dell customer.

Dell's penchant for tracking every last detail can land him in hot water. On October 10, during the trial of former Credit Suisse First Boston technology banker Frank P. Quattrone for allegedly obstructing an investigation into the bank's handling of hot initial public offerings, prosecutors revealed e-mails between Dell and Quattrone. In one July 2000 exchange, Dell requested 250,000 shares in Corvis Corp., a promising networking company that was preparing to go public, for his corporate venture-capital fund. Dell suggested that the allocation "would certainly help" the relationship between his company and CSFB. Dell declined to comment. But his spokesperson says that he was merely trying to assist the fund and noted that the company did not do any investment-banking business with CSFB before or after the exchange. In a separate e-mail on which Michael Dell was copied, the manager of Dell's personal venture fund requested Corvis shares for the fund. A spokesperson for that fund says that it had invested in Corvis in 1999 and that there was nothing improper about the request.

Rollins has the same attention to detail as Michael Dell. He is overseeing a Six Sigma transformation of everything from manufacturing to marketing that is expected to help cut expenses $1.5 billion this year. The emphasis is on small surgical strikes on defects and waste, not massive restructurings. Consider a Six Sigma meeting one balmy July afternoon. Rollins listened to John Holland, a technician in Dell's server factory, describe how his team replaced the colored paper it used to print out parts lists with plain white paper, saving $23,000. "Where else do you get a supervisor making $40,000 a year presenting to the president of a $40 billion company?" says Americas Operations Vice President Dick Hunter, Holland's boss.

The discipline in Michael Dell's management style is most apparent in the way the company approaches new markets. Take Dell's plunge into the $50 billion printer business. Beginning in 2001, a team of Dell strategists spent more than a year researching the market. Dell started serious planning only after finding that nearly two-thirds of its customers said that they would buy a Dell printer if they could get the same kind of service they got when they bought a PC or a server. In the summer of 2002, Vice President Tim Peters, a veteran of Dell's handheld launch, was tapped to lead the effort. But like any executive planning to put out a new product, he had to face the gauntlet of Dell and Rollins. After thinking up a strategy, he had to sit by while it was picked apart.

Nothing was left to chance. Dell prodded Peters to think about product features and the buying experience, while Rollins pushed him to keep costs low without sacrificing quality. Both bosses wanted to make sure that the timing was right. That required intense discussions about how standardized printer technologies were and the state of the supply chain that Dell would use. One key challenge: ink. Customers typically buy replacement cartridges at a nearby retailer. It didn't seem likely that they would wait for days for an Internet order from Dell to arrive.

The toughest task in any product launch is the math. At Dell, a new line of PCs, which is good for $2 billion to $3 billion in annual revenue, costs roughly $10 million to launch. Any new idea must have a comparable return, says G. Carl Everett, a Dell senior vice president who retired in 2001, and turn a profit from the get-go. That's what Peters had to promise in printers. The rare exceptions occur only when Dell senses an opportunity that's critical to the company's future. Dell's server business, for instance, took 18 months to reach profitability, says former Vice President Michael D. Lambert.

In the printer business, it took seven months for Peters to work everything out. The products debuted in March and were profitable immediately. Peters's proposed solution to the ink riddle: every Dell printer comes loaded with software directing users to Dell.com, where they can order a new cartridge and have it delivered the next day. Still, Michael Dell never let up: the night before the launch, he sat up until 2 a.m. to watch the printers debut online and then zipped e-mails to Peters with suggestions for improvement. When initial sales came in at double the internal target, Peters's team got a very Dell-like reward: a quick trip to see *Terminator 3*.

That flick may turn out to have more than therapeutic value, considering that rival HP is determined to wipe out Dell's printer ambitions. HP's strategy is to leave Dell in the dust with a burst of innovation. It spends $1 billion a year on printer research—more than twice Dell's entire R&D budget. HP is using that money to develop products like high-end photo ink that will last 73 years, nearly 10 times as long as what Dell offers. "Dell is going to hit a wall," says Jeff Clarke, HP's executive vice president for global operations. "We view them as low-tech and low-cost. They're the Kmart of the industry." And some experts say that Dell won't threaten HP's 60 percent market share anytime soon. Gartner Inc. estimates that Dell claimed less than 1 percent of the printer market in the second quarter, mostly at the low end of the business.

ATTACKING FROM BELOW

If past experience is any guide, Dell may struggle as it tries to move upmarket. With its bare-bones R&D budget, it had to kill off high-end servers that go head-to-head with fancy gear from Sun, saying that the soft demand didn't merit its attention. And after two and a half years selling networking gear, Dell has failed to deliver products powerful enough to threaten Cisco Systems Inc.'s dominant market share. Yet Dell is betting that as technology improves, the low-end products that it sells so deftly will become more than good enough for most customers, leaving its rivals scrambling to find their next high-end innovation. "The history of the industry is [that] the attack from below works," says Merrill Lynch's Milunovich.

Indeed, Dell has had no trouble gobbling up sales as markets mature. In storage, its sales now account for 10 percent of EMC's revenue, some $600 million annually. In the low-margin home-PC market, which Dell long avoided, unit sales have grown an average of 46 percent in the past four quarters.

Michael Dell certainly would take exception to HP's jabs about his company being the Kmart of technology. But there are some striking similarities between Dell and another giant retailer: Wal-Mart. Like the behemoth from Bentonville, Arkansas, Dell has built a business as a superefficient distributor, with the tightly run operations and thrifty management to enter any number of new markets quickly and easily. "We've always toyed with the idea that we could distribute anything," says Morton L. Topfer, a former Dell vice chairman who now sits on the company's board. Maybe not anything. But Dell is striving to greatly expand his reach in the technology world. With his management philosophy of constant improvement, he seems to be well on his way.

UPDATE
Despite Michael Dell's improvement efforts, Dell has continued to have problems with customer satisfaction, batteries, and earnings.

THE PROBLEM

Achieving high growth, even as lower-cost competitors imitate your superior supply chain and efficient distribution

Entering new markets without distinctive product innovations

Motivating employees without the adrenalin rush or "underdog" identity of a start-up

THE SOLUTION

Expand into higher-growth markets, where speed and execution are the keys to success.

Communicate honestly to your team about your weaknesses and explore potential changes in management style.

SUSTAINING THE WIN

Be wary of faster innovators in new markets, especially as wireless technology takes off.

MICHAEL ESKEW: UPS AND BIG BROWN'S NEW BAG

Courtesy of Getty Images.

POWER PLAYER
CEO Michael Eskew is betting UPS's fortunes on its ability to redefine itself yet again. This time the legendary shipper is entrenching itself even more deeply with its customers and becoming a true supply-chain partner.

In Dean Foust's 2004 profile, UPS sets its sights on becoming the traffic manager for Corporate America.

LESSON PLAN

Set your company on course to win—even if its new strategy requires lowering profit margins.

Transform a conservative corporate culture into one that embraces taking calculated risks—and excels by doing so.

Adapt or perish. Continuous reinvention will keep you one step ahead of new inventions and technologies that can make your product obsolete.

A COURSE TO WIN

For years, the bane of most Ford dealers was the automaker's Rube Goldberg–like system for getting cars from factory to showroom. Cars could take as long as a month to arrive—that is, when they weren't lost along the way. And Ford Motor Co. was not always able to tell its dealers exactly what was coming, or even what was in inventory at the nearest rail yards. "We'd lose track of whole trainloads of cars," recalls Jerry Reynolds, owner of Prestige Ford in Garland, Texas. "It was crazy."

But three years ago, Ford handed over its byzantine distribution network to an unlikely source for an overhaul: United Parcel Service Inc. In a joint venture with the carmaker, UPS engineers, with input from Reynolds and other dealers, redesigned Ford's entire North American delivery network, streamlining everything from the route cars take from the factory to how they're processed at regional sorting hubs. Ultimately, UPS deployed a tracking system similar to the one it uses to monitor 13.8 million packages daily—right down to slapping bar codes on the windshields of the 4 million cars rolling out of Ford's 19 North American plants and onto railcars each year.

The result: UPS has cut the time that it takes autos to arrive at dealer lots by 40 percent, to 10 days on average. That saves Ford millions in working capital each year and makes it easy for its 6,500 dealers to track down the models that are most in demand. [General Motors Corp., by contrast, uses a proprietary online system for distribution; Chrysler Corp. contracts with Union Pacific Corp.] "It was the most amazing transformation I had ever seen," marvels Reynolds. "My last comment to UPS was: 'Can you get us spare parts like this?'"

REINVENTING—ONCE AGAIN

Welcome to the new UPS. Ever since its humble beginnings in 1907 as a Seattle messenger service, the real story about UPS has been how this traditionally insular and conservative enterprise has managed to reinvent itself time and again to keep growing. No matter how dangerous the next step might have seemed, UPS took it. Back when the telephone became a household staple, founder James E. Casey remade his messenger service into a home delivery business for retailers. When Americans began buying cars and driving their purchases home, UPS reinvented itself again, fighting scores of legal battles so that its fleet could compete with the U.S. Postal Service.

Those moves have helped make UPS into the colossus it is today. In 2003, Big Brown earned $2.9 billion on $33.5 billion in revenues. And its stock, at about $74, has outperformed the market since the company went public in November 1999. In 2004, UPS shares have generated total shareholder returns of 21 percent, compared with a negative 12 percent return for the Standard & Poor's 500-stock index.

ASSESS, DEVELOP, AND EXECUTE

To keep up the momentum, UPS is undergoing its latest makeover. With its U.S. delivery business maturing, the company has been working feverishly to transform itself into a logistics expert. Last year, that end of the business accounted for $2.1 billion in revenues, or just 6 percent of the UPS total. But analysts believe that logistics could provide a potentially huge new revenue stream—up to 20 percent of future growth by some estimates. Simply put, UPS wants to leverage decades of experience managing its own global delivery network to serve as the traffic manager for Corporate America's sprawling distribution networks, doing everything from scheduling the planes, trains, and ships on which goods move to owning and managing companies' distribution centers and warehouses. Just as important, says UPS, is that its strategy should also generate additional delivery business for its ubiquitous brown trucks and private air fleet. The pitch to customers: let us manage the supply chain, while you focus on core marketing and product development. That way, says CEO Michael L. Eskew, 55, UPS can help companies "improve their cash flow, their customer service, and their productivity."

POWER MOVE

In order to stay ahead, UPS has found it necessary to assess, develop, and execute— again and again. As competitors, customers, and market dynamics change, winning companies never stop asking, "What business are we in?" From messenger company to package delivery service, UPS has continuously redefined itself, and today it is in the business of "enabling commerce around the globe."

If its new strategy succeeds, UPS will gain much more than a revenue stream. As a partner (rather than only a vendor), UPS has visibility into the inner workings of its customers: economics, marketing, and operations. With these critical pieces of information, UPS can do more to win—by ensuring that its customers win first.

LOGISTICS BRING REVENUE AND PARTNERS

This shift in focus is not without risks for UPS. Contract logistics is historically a lower-margin business than package delivery. Analysts estimate that the company's operating margins in logistics are only 5 percent overall. Although large-scale consulting contracts can be quite profitable, bread-and-butter work like freight forwarding, managing warehouses, or order fulfillment can earn as little as 2 percent. Margins on the company's core delivery business, on the other hand, hover around 15 percent. "The dilemma with logistics is that it offers high revenue growth, but if you aren't careful, minimal profit growth," warns Morgan Stanley (JPM) analyst James Valentine.

Some big rivals question whether UPS can generate enough additional delivery business to justify its foray into logistics. "The contract logistics business is fundamentally low margin," says FedEx Corp. Chairman Frederick W. Smith. "And I'm not sure the fundamental premise—that it will result in you getting more profitable small-shipment business—is correct."

But UPS maintains that it is already seeing such a payoff. Indeed, some analysts estimate that in 2003 UPS used logistics to snag an extra $2 billion in shipping volume. UPS executives also maintain that because logistics is far less capital-intensive than the delivery business—with its heavy investments in trucks, airplanes, technology, and real estate—logistics has a high return on investment. And they contend that the margins will improve as the business grows.

For now, UPS is taking on more and more contracts where its brown trucks aren't involved—or where they come into play only at the end of the journey. Consider its deal with Birkenstock Footprint Sandals Inc. UPS contracts with ocean carriers to get shoes made in Germany across the Atlantic to New Jersey ports, instead of routing them through the Panama Canal to the shoemaker's California warehouses. Each incoming shipment is whisked away to a UPS distribution hub and, within hours, to retailers. By handing over its keys to UPS, Birkenstock has cut the time it takes to get shoes to stores by half, to just three weeks. "Our spring fashion merchandise shipped 100 percent on time—and it was the first time in history I've been able to say that," says Birkenstock's chief operating officer, Gene Kunde.

INDISPENSABLE TO CUSTOMERS

In fact, there seem to be few tasks that UPS won't undertake in order to embed itself with customers. For Jockey International Inc., UPS not only manages a warehouse but also handles Internet order fulfillment. Apparel bought on the Jockey Web site is boxed for shipping by UPS warehouse staffers and delivered by UPS drivers. And if there's a problem, calls are handled by UPS phone reps. Big Brown also handles laptop repairs for Toshiba America, installs x-ray machines in Europe for Philips Medical Systems, and dresses Teddy bears for TeddyCrafters.

The UPS move is partly defensive. Today a growing breed of consultants uses sophisticated computer programs to help corporate clients negotiate aggressive shipping discounts. And shipping rivals such as Deutsche Post, with its DHL unit, are aggressively moving into logistics. In recent years, DHL and FedEx have nibbled away at UPS's domestic ground business—since 1998, its market share had shrunk from 57.7 percent to 56.9 percent. "We had a legitimate fear of becoming a commodity and having other providers deal with our customers," says James P. Kelly, who retired as the CEO of UPS in 2001 but remains a director. "If we didn't do it, someone else was going to."

> **POWER MOVE**
>
> Order fulfillment brings UPS closer to its customers, which is critical to the success of its new strategy. However, UPS must not lose focus on its core capabilities—transportation and logistics. Succeeding in that low-margin, competitive industry will be challenging enough.

Logistics represents a personal crusade of sorts for Eskew. A UPS careerist, he began formulating such a move several years ago when he served as head of strategic planning. But it wasn't until a management retreat in early 2002, where senior executives were pondering whether the company needed to expand into manufacturing or some other field to sustain its long-term growth, that Eskew convinced them that logistics was the answer. But doing it well, cautioned Eskew, would force UPS to reinvent itself yet again. "We can play a significant role [in logistics], but we will have to change ourselves," he said.

POWER MOVE

Eskew's emphasis on culture is critical. Too often, executives try to steer companies in new directions, but forget that neglecting to reinvent the corporate culture can cause even the best-laid plans to fail.

DON'T LOSE FOCUS ON CORE BUSINESS—CULTURE IS CRITICAL

Since the year 2000, UPS has spent more than $1 billion to buy 25 companies involved in freight forwarding, customs clearance, finance, and other logistics services. Eskew pulled some rising UPS stars from the mainstay delivery operations and put them on to his new supply-chain team. And in a departure from the cautious UPS culture, Eskew pushed managers to take risks, counseling that failure wasn't irreparable as long as you "fail quick and fail small."

To its credit, UPS has learned how to keep those small failures from getting bigger. According to former executives, a UPS deal to acquire San Francisco's Fritz Cos., a freight forwarder that contracts with various carriers to help companies move goods, didn't go smoothly. After Fritz's entrepreneurial staffers clashed with by-the-book UPS managers, many left. That led to the defection of key customers like giant Costco Wholesale Corp. (COST). But in time, UPS stabilized Fritz's operations, installed some of its own managers, and lured back clients: Costco began using UPS freight forwarding again earlier this year.

Eskew can now turn his attention to convincing the rest of Corporate America that UPS isn't just about parcels anymore; it's the missing link that can make their supply chains stronger. And if that pitch also helps UPS lock up their shipping business, so much the better.

MONDAY MORNING...

THE PROBLEM
Moving an industry titan into new territory without sacrificing too much market share in existing businesses

THE SOLUTION
Leverage the company's core capabilities to bring it closer to its customers.

SUSTAINING THE WIN
Choose the right talent to execute, making sure these individuals can also champion the culture change.

MORNING

EDWARD ZANDER:
MOTOROLA SHAKE UP

©Erik S. Lesser/Bloomberg News.

Transform a dysfunctional corporate culture into one that values performance and collaboration.

Design incentive plans that reward collaboration, not just individual bottom-line unit performance.

Realign formerly automonous business units to encourage agility.

POWER PLAYER

Soon after Ed Zander stepped into his new role as the CEO of Motorola, he made it clear that things would change. To win with his new strategy, he has to change the focus, cadence, and even the shape of Motorola as he shakes things up in a bid to make the company a tech leader.

In 2004, Roger O. Crockett dug out the details of new CEO Edward Zander's shakeup plans a week before Zander went public with them.

A SENSE OF URGENCY

It takes Motorola Inc. employees about 30 seconds after they meet Edward J. Zander to realize how different their new boss is from their last one. Where Zander's predecessor, Christopher B. Galvin, was reserved, polite, and genteel, Zander is a brash Brooklynite, incessantly pumping hands and flashing his trademark mile-wide smile.

But three months after taking over the chief executive post, Zander showed that he also was going to be much more demanding. He gathered his top 20 executives in the company's downtown Chicago offices, some 30 miles from the Schaumburg, Illinois, headquarters, for a two-day brainstorming session on how to improve Motorola's lackluster execution.

Zander's message: employees will be held accountable for customer satisfaction, product quality, and even collaboration among business units. "If you don't cooperate and work together, I will kill you," he said. Today, Zander laughs: "That's surviving-and-growing-up-in-Brooklyn talk. It was my way of saying, 'We're going to fix this thing.'"

POWER MOVE

A powerful strategy does not just define what a company produces, but also articulates a clear benefit for the customer—in this case, helping end users achieve "seamless mobility." Far more effective than a laundry list of discrete initiatives (which can seem like assignments to employees), a compelling vision for success creates a stronger motivation: a set of shared goals.

Zander is about as affable as CEOs come, but he's deadly serious about returning Motorola to the top of the communications world. The tech veteran, who spent 15 years at computer giant Sun Microsystems Inc. and eventually became its president, is trying to reinvent Motorola as a nimble, unified technology company. His most dramatic effort to date is a plan to dismantle Motorola's debilitating bureaucracy and end a culture of internecine rivalries so intense that Motorola's own employees have referred to its business units as "warring tribes." And he's not leaving it to chance: he has made cooperation a key factor in determining raises and bonuses. "It's a damn different place," says Patrick J. Canavan, a 24-year veteran and Motorola's director for global governance. "Everyone is looking out for everyone else."

The changes are just beginning. Zander has been exploring a major reorganization, and the first steps of this restructuring were unveiled at an investor conference in Chicago on July 27, 2004. By October 2004, Zander hoped to abandon Motorola's stovepipe divisions, which are focused on products like mobile phones and broadband gear, and reorganize operations around customer markets—one for the digital home, for example, and another for corporate buyers.

SEAMLESS MOBILITY

The reorganization will help Zander deliver on several new initiatives. Perhaps the most important is what the chief executive calls "seamless mobility." The idea is that Motorola should make it easy for consumers to transport any digital information—music, video, e-mail, phone calls—from the house to the car to the workplace. Mastering that technology would do more than boost cell phone sales. It also could make Motorola a key player in the digital home, helping it sell flat-panel TVs and broadband modems, home wireless networks, and gateways to manage digital content. Separately, *BusinessWeek* has learned that Motorola is planning a major push to sell more services to corporations. While Motorola sells communications gear to corporate customers now, Zander sees an important growth opportunity in managing networks for those companies. "We have to get more focused on that," said Zander in an interview with *BusinessWeek*.

POWER MOVE

In a way, Motorola's new strategy is risky. If it succeeds, consumers will outfit their homes with a fleet of Motorola products and services, and the cost to switch to another provider will be high—much to Motorola's advantage. But, if any of its products—say, the modem—is substandard, a consumer may choose another brand entirely, even if the rest of Motorola's gadgets are superior.

So far, Motorola is performing impressively under its new chief executive. On July 20, the company reported that second-quarter sales surged 41 percent, to $8.7 billion, while operating income rose fivefold, to $845 million. The primary driver was the mobile-phone division, which boosted revenues 67 percent, to $3.9 billion. Still, investors are looking for Motorola to get its profitability up to the level of its rivals. Despite Nokia Corp.'s recent troubles, the operating margins in its mobile-phone business are 19 percent, compared with 10 percent for Motorola. "Margins are still subpar," says Barbara L. Rishel, a senior portfolio manager for MTB Investment Advisors, a large Motorola shareholder.

POWER MOVE

Major shifts in strategy often require organizational change. In particular, strategies that require collaboration among business units cannot succeed if the organization—structure and systems—gets in the way. With Motorola's history of internal strife, fewer business units means fewer opportunities for turf wars.

HONING A CONCEPT

There's no disagreement with that from Zander. Although he's unlikely to announce it on July 27, Zander is planning to trim costs in coming months by shedding employees, according to insiders and analysts. He's also plotting management changes that will bring in more handpicked people to help execute his plans. On July 20, Motorola said that the head of its mobile-phone division, Tom Lynch, would leave the company at the end of the summer. Zander declined to discuss any details of cost cutting or executive changes.

But investors who want Zander to jettison poorly performing businesses may be disappointed. The CEO proceeded with the spin-off of Motorola's semiconductor unit, which had been put in motion before he arrived—the deal took place on July 16, despite upheaval in the chips market. Still, insiders say that he's impressed with the remaining portfolio of businesses, including the $4.4 billion wireless infrastructure business that some analysts have suggested that Motorola dump.

Instead, Zander is focused on reducing the number of separate businesses. Analysts say that he is working on a plan that could combine the wireless network unit with the company's broadband division. By combining two units that make equipment to route data through networks, Motorola could cut expenses and smooth execution. Zander declined to comment on any potential reorganization.

Just as important as the structural changes will be the strategy that goes with them. The concept of seamless mobility was born on a flight to France in February, when Zander and his chief technology officer, Padmasree Warrior, were headed to a wireless-industry conference. The strategy has been refined over the past few months until senior leaders from Motorola's business units gathered last month at Motorola University, adjacent to headquarters, to discuss strategies for internal development and potential acquisitions.

EXECUTION, EXECUTION, EXECUTION

The Motorola vision starts with users sitting at home watching, say, the New York Yankees battling the Chicago White Sox. To leave home, they pause the video, transfer it to their phone, walk into the garage, and transfer the video to the car's system as they drive away. The car's controls would switch to audio so as not to distract the driver and then switch back to video when the driver stops at a traffic light. Motorola has the technology portfolio to pursue the entire scenario. Besides phones and cable set-top boxes, it has a $2.3 billion automotive-electronics business that develops technologies for cars to communicate with outside networks.

The key to success will be beating rivals to market with innovative solutions. That's why Zander's top priority has been improving execution. The main driver is a new incentive plan. In the past, workers were compensated based on the revenue, profit, and cash generated in their particular sector. If one sector did well, its employees pulled in huge bonuses. A unit that didn't perform got little or nothing.

Zander has been relentless in trying to get the most out of his staff. A new plan bases 25 percent of the bonus on three key areas: customer satisfaction, product reliability, and the cost of poor quality. When the heads of each business unit first laid out their targets, Zander's no-nonsense roots showed: "You're sandbagging," he barked. Before long, the targets were more

POWER MOVE

The success of Zander's new strategy depends on a new corporate culture, including operating routines and decision-making processes. Although both can be partially managed through effective incentive plans, Zander must continue to lead by example if the company is to sustain any long-term change.

difficult. "We're driving for improvement year over year," says Michael J. Fenger, a vet whom Zander picked to improve corporate quality.

If Zander can maintain Motorola's momentum, the years ahead look promising. It's gaining share on the world's mobile-phone leader, Nokia, and the elements of Zander's master plan have yet to take root. "It's a big ship," Zander concedes—so it will take time to change direction. But it takes no time at all to see that Zander is committed to the challenge.

THE PROBLEM
Low-growth business units and a destructive corporate culture

THE SOLUTION
Set a vision for the future, and improve execution so as to achieve it.

SUSTAINING THE WIN
Put your money where your mouth is. Measure what needs to be managed.

Establish systems to reassess strategy, organization, and culture—and readjust them if necessary.

SAM PALMISANO:
IBM AND THE NEW BLUE

©Brad Trent

Empower your employees to develop a unifying, motivating strategy that can move the company back to the top.

Take bold, decisive action to create an organization and culture that fit the new strategy and operating model.

POWER PLAYER

As IBM's new CEO, Sam Palmisano was stepping into the shoes of one of the world's most famous leaders. To make his mark, Palmisano was leading IBM with an ambitious strategy to develop the technology platform of the future: e-business on demand.

Spencer Ante's profiles from 2003 IBM's boss as he wraps up his first year on the job.

BOLD MOVES

The directors were just sitting down for the first IBM board meeting of the year on January 28, 2003, when CEO Samuel J. Palmisano dropped a bombshell. For years, the board had lavished wealth upon Louis V. Gerstner Jr., keeping his pay in line with that of other pinstriped superstars across Corporate America. But in a surprise break from the past, Palmisano asked the board to cut his 2003 bonus and set it aside as a pool of money to be shared by about 20 top executives based on their performance as a team. Palmisano doesn't want to say how much he's pitching in, but insiders say it's $3 to $5 million—nearly half his bonus.

A crowd-pleasing gesture? It was just his latest salvo. Five days earlier, he took aim at a bastion of power and privilege at Big Blue, the 92-year-old executive management committee. For generations, this 12-person body presiding over IBM's strategy and initiatives represented the inner sanctum for every aspiring Big Blue executive. Palmisano himself was anointed back in 1997, a promotion that signaled the shimmering possibilities ahead. But on January 23, the CEO hit the send button on an e-mail to 300 senior managers announcing that this venerable committee was finito, kaput. Instead, Palmisano would work directly with three teams he had put in place the year before—teams that included people from all over the company who could bring the best ideas to the table. The old committee, with its monthly meetings, just slowed things down.

All the while, Palmisano was piecing together an audacious program to catapult IBM back to the zenith of technology. It started at an August 5 strategy meeting, when he asked his team to draw up a project as epochal as the mainframe computer—IBM's big bet from 40 years ago. During the day, the team cobbled together a vision of systems that would alter the very nature of how technology is delivered. IBM would supply computing power as if it were water or electricity. But how to tackle a project this vast? No one knew where to begin. A frustrated Palmisano abruptly cut short the meeting and gave the team 90 days to assemble and launch the megaproject. Three months later, the CEO unveiled "e-business on demand." Standing in New York's American Museum of Natural History, not far from the hulking dinosaurs whose fate IBM had narrowly skirted,

Palmisano vowed to lead a new world of computing. "We have an opportunity to set the agenda in our industry," he says.

BACK TO THE FUTURE

After one year on the job, Palmisano is putting his imprint on the company—and with a vengeance. Sure, IBM roared back to strength in the late 1990s. But Palmisano is out to remake the company and hoist it back to greatness. Through much of the twentieth century, under the leadership of Thomas J. Watson and his son, Thomas, Jr., IBM not only ruled computing and defined the American multinational but was the gold standard for corporations. From the days of tabulating machines all the way to the Space Age, when its mainframes helped chart the path to the moon, IBM was a paragon of power, prestige, and farsightedness. It was tops in technology, but it was also a leader in bringing women and minorities into a well-paid workforce and in creating a corporate culture that inspired lifelong loyalty. "We stood for something back then," Palmisano says.

To return IBM to greatness, the 51-year-old Palmisano is turning the company inside out. He's the first true-blue IBMer to take the reins since the company's fall from grace more than a decade ago. And while the new CEO never criticizes his predecessor, who rescued IBM and pushed many key technologies, Palmisano is quietly emerging as the antithesis of Gerstner. Where Gerstner raked in money, Palmisano makes a point of splitting the booty with his team. While Gerstner ruled IBM regally, Palmisano is egalitarian. The revolution he is leading spells the end of the imperial CEO at IBM. "Creativity in any large organization does not come from one individual, the celebrity CEO," Palmisano says. "That stuff's B.S. Creativity in an organization starts where the action is—either in the laboratory, or in R&D sites, at a customer place, in manufacturing."

If that sounds like the IBM of old, that's exactly what Palmisano is hoping for. The flattening of the organization, the lowering of CEO pay, the emphasis on teams—it's all part of his broad campaign to return to IBM's roots. Palmisano believes that core values remain in what he calls the company's DNA, waiting to be awakened. And he thinks that this message, which might have elicited chortles during the tech boom, resonates in the wake of the market crash and

Even the best-laid strategy will fail without the right organizational structure and culture. A hierarchical, command-and-control model fits an organization whose primary purpose is speedy, flawless execution, but IBM requires a flatter, more egalitarian organization to provide a risk-free environment in which people will feel comfortable offering bold, unconventional ideas.

corporate scandals. More important, he believes that only by returning to what made IBM great can the company rise to resume its place of leadership in America and the world.

GO WHERE THE MARKET'S GOING

At the heart of Palmisano's plan is e-business on demand. This project, which is already gobbling up a third of IBM's $5 billion research and development budget, puts Big Blue in the vanguard of a massive computing shift. The company is starting by helping customers standardize all their computing needs. Then, in the course of the next 10 years, it plans to handle growing amounts of this work on its own massive computer grids. And this won't be just techie grunt work. The eventual goal is to imbue these systems with deep industrial expertise so that IBM is not only crunching numbers and dispatching e-mails, but also delivering technology that helps companies solve thorny technical problems—from testing drugs to simulating car crashes. It's a soaring vision. But Palmisano has believers. "Sam is aiming to go where the market's going, not to where it's been," says Cisco Systems Inc. CEO John Chambers.

The obstacles he faces are immense. Start with the technology. The vision of on-demand computing is downright audacious. It proposes joining all of the thousands of computers and applications in enormous enterprises and getting them to work seamlessly and in unison—not only in-house, but with partners and customers. Assembling the pieces will require every bit of IBM's vaunted smarts, and a scrap of luck as well. IBM officials say that only 10 percent of the technology needed for this system is ready. And many of the necessary pieces, including futuristic software programs that will heal themselves, are at the basic test stage in IBM's labs. "There are huge, huge technical challenges," says A. Richard Newton, dean of the College of Engineering at the University of California at Berkeley.

Palmisano faces an equally imposing job at home. To make good on his vision, he must turn IBM itself into a user of on-demand computing and become a prototype for its customers. This entails recharting the path of every bit of information flowing inside the company. It means not just shifting the computer systems, but redefining nearly everyone's job. And if IBM meets resistance to these changes, it could stumble in producing the new technology. This could undermine IBM's $800 million marketing campaign for e-business on demand—and scare away customers in droves. Such a failure could punish IBM financially, forcing a retreat toward fiercely competitive markets such as servers and chips. "The two most important parts of their business—services and software—are tied to the [on-demand] strategy," says Gartner analyst Tom Bittman. "They need to succeed."

Is history on Palmisano's side? Try to think of a great technology company that took a life-threatening fall and then scratched and clawed all the way back to the very top. Westinghouse? Digital Equipment ? Xerox ? Some have survived. But if Palmisano leads IBM back to the summit, Big Blue will be the first full-fledged round-tripper.

MOVE FAST

To get there, he must win a brutal battle raging among the titans of tech. From Hewlett-Packard Co. to Microsoft Corp. , the industry's bruisers are all pushing research into next-generation computing systems that will rival IBM's. Big Blue appears to be better positioned than its foes, thanks to a wider range of offerings. But, warns Irving Wladawsky-Berger, IBM's general manager for e-business on demand: "In 1996, we had the benefit of being considered irrelevant. [Microsoft's William H.] Gates and [Steven A.] Ballmer felt pity for us. Now they are all watching us. If we don't move fast, they will pass us."

The new initiative provides Palmisano with a prodigious tool to remake the company. Gerstner's reforms began the process, directing IBM toward software and services. But Palmisano's e-business on demand goes much further. It extends into nearly every nook of Big Blue, from its sales force and its army of systems consultants to the big brains cooking up the software code in the research and development labs. Management expert Jim Collins, author of *Good to Great*, says that Palmisano's willingness to think and act boldly bodes well and recalls earlier outsize bets in IBM's history, such as the development of the tabulating machine. "It reminds me of what Tom Watson Sr. did during the Depression," he says.

Palmisano already is banking on winning his share of the new business. Last year IBM saw revenue slip 2 percent, to $81.2 billion, with earnings tumbling 54 percent, to $3.6 billion. But this year Palmisano is counting on e-business on demand to fuel the hottest sales growth at Big Blue since 1995. Analysts predict 9 percent revenue growth this year. And Palmisano expects 40 percent of this—nearly $3 billion—to come from new offerings in e-business on demand. These include servers running the free Linux operating system and grid software that pools the power of scores of networked computers into a virtual supercomputer.

By pursuing this plan, Palmisano is fleeing the brutish world of hardware and seeking refuge in profitable software and services businesses. He bulked up for this drive last year by spending $3.5 billion for PricewaterhouseCoopers Consulting and another $2.1 billion for Rational Software Corp., a maker of software tools to write programs. And why not? According to IBM's internal research, 60 percent of the profits in the $1 trillion high-tech industry will come from software and services by 2005. That's up from 45 percent in 2002. "We're just going where the profit is," Palmisano says.

POWER MOVE

Globalization has made it difficult for traditional multinational companies to compete in manufacturing-based businesses, such as hardware. As soon as IBM develops the new ThinkPad, a faster, lower-cost competitor from an emerging market will begin producing it for less. Both software and service businesses require creativity, subtlety, and flexible thinking—characteristics that are much less easily imitated than the design of a hard drive.

LEADERSHIP AND TEAMWORK FROM ALL LEVELS

And he's leading Big Blue in a way it has never been led before. One year before Palmisano disbanded the Executive Management Committee, he had put in place his management teams for the future. He created three of them: strategy, operations, and technology. Instead of picking only high-level executives for each team, Palmisano selected the managers and engineers who were most familiar with the issues. "Heads are spinning," says J. Bruce Harreld, senior vice president for strategy. "He's reaching six levels down and asking questions."

Talk to Palmisano for an hour and he'll mention teamwork 20 times. His entire on-demand strategy hinges upon it. Why? For IBM to come up with a broad array of on-demand technologies in a hurry, the whole company has to work smoothly from one far-flung cubicle to another. That means bringing researchers in touch not only with product developers, but with consultants and even customers. Only by reaching across these old boundaries will IBM be able to find out what its customers are clamoring for—and produce it fast.

To head up this process, Palmisano has chosen Irving Wladawsky-Berger, the renowned Cuban-born computer scientist who was IBM's e-business guru in the 1990s. Today, Wladawsky-Berger's mission is to drive the strategy across the company. In the last two months, he has assembled 28 people working in every division of IBM into what he calls a "virtual team." These are Wladawsky-Berger's on-demand agents. They nose around their areas of expertise, looking for on-demand possibilities. New servers coming out later this year, for example, will be equipped to dispatch excess work to other machines on the network.

Still, coaxing separate divisions to dance in unison is no easy job. Clashes are common, for example, when IBM's 160,000 Global Service workers descend into the research labs. Last year, researchers were hard at work on a program for supply chains in the electronics industry. Consultants ordered a quick version of the same program for a car maker. The two sides battled briefly until the researchers adapted a program for cars then went back to work on electronics. The consultants' time frame, says William Grey, manager of IBM's Finance Research, "is milliseconds. Ours is five years. There's a cultural gap that needs to be bridged."

SHOW THEM YOU'RE SERIOUS

The key is getting IBM itself to function as an e-business-on-demand enterprise. To drive this message through the company, Palmisano in January grabbed a star manager, Linda Sanford, and put her in charge of internal e-business on demand. Sanford, a senior vice president, had revived IBM's storage business and was viewed as a bona fide up-and-comer at Big Blue. "I take a senior vice president who has a great job, and say, 'O.K., you're going to make IBM on demand,'" Palmisano says. "Then, 320,000 people say, 'Holy . . ., this guy's serious.'"

By implementing e-business on demand in his own company first, Palmisano achieves two things. First, he enables his employees to understand the ins and outs of this complex, ambitious plan. Second, he communicates to the market that this strategy will win, and that IBM will compete fiercely until it does.

Sanford faces an imposing job. First, she has to supervise the overhaul of IBM's massive supply chain. That means piling $44 billion of purchases into a single system. It's a slog. It means pushing IBM's engineers to switch to company-approved suppliers. Then a procurement rep is assigned to each development team to make sure that all the teams use industry-standard parts. It's intrusive. But like the rest of the on-demand program, it focuses the company on a single effort. And it should pay dividends. Palmisano expects the entire initiative to yield 5 percent productivity gains, worth $2 to $3 billion a year, for the next five to ten years.

Sanford also is working to create an online inventory of IBM's knowledge. She's turning the company's intranet into a giant collaboration portal. One feature is an "expertise locator" that helps an employee find, say, a software engineer with expertise in building databases in Linux. But at a meeting of the operations team at Armonk, New York, on a cold mid-February morning, a frustrated Sanford told key executives, including Palmisano, that the concept was a hard sell.

LEAD BY EXAMPLE

Palmisano, his face cupped in his hands, looked concerned. "There's a huge level of expectation on this portal," he said. "I just hope we can deliver." Sanford responded with a blunt message: if Palmisano wants the portal to succeed, he and his teams must lead by example, offering their own areas of expertise within a 30-day deadline. "We have to lead the way," she said.

For Palmisano, this means rallying the biggest brains and deepest thinkers in the company to the cause. In January he flew to Harvard University in Cambridge for a meeting with IBM's top computer scientists. His message was simple and straightforward: the dream of on-demand computing hinged on their ability to produce technology breakthroughs.

While scientists are wrestling with future iterations of on-demand computing, IBM's sales team is rolling out the first products. New IBM servers include a feature called *hypervisors*. These allow technicians to monitor as many as 100 servers at a time, shifting work from one machine to another. A new program from IBM's Tivoli group performs similar work; it patrols the network, constantly on the lookout for servers that are running short of memory. When it finds one, it automatically shifts the work to other computers. This is a key aspect of on-demand computing, and a potential money saver. Once systems can distribute work, companies will be able to run their servers at a higher level, much closer to capacity. This reduces costs. And if work piles up, customers will ship excess tasks to IBM.

Many of these customers, IBM hopes, will eventually leave the computing business altogether and ship all their digital work to IBM. American Express likes the idea. A year ago, before Palmisano even came up with the new vision, AmEx signed a seven-year, $4 billion services contract with Big Blue. At first blush, it looks like a standard outsourcing deal; the company has shifted its computers and 2,000 tech employees to IBM. But what makes it different is the economics. AmEx pays only for the technology it uses every month. The advantages? AmEx is looking to save hundreds of millions of dollars over the course of the contract. And with IBM running the system, says Glen Salow, chief information officer at American Express, "they can upgrade technology five times faster."

DO MORE WITH LESS

Palmisano's vision for e-business on demand stretches beyond the technical challenges to the realm of human knowledge. In the services division, IBM has experts on industries ranging from banking to metals to autos. He wants to gather their know-how—"deep process insights," he calls it—into the systems. Eventually, he sees IBM's on-demand offerings reinventing the company's corporate customers and shaking up entire industries.

POWER MOVE

As populations grow, winning companies will be those that successfully do more with less through creative technology solutions, clever process fixes, or some combination of the two.

IBM is developing 17 different industrial road maps for on demand. Pharmaceuticals is one. There, a computer grid will handle simulation and modeling to reduce the number of clinical trials needed. That, IBM says, could lead to improving the success rates of

Palmisano's e-business strategy will bring IBM closer to its customers. Like Amazon and UPS, IBM aims to establish itself as a critical partner to its clients, not only to fine-tune its own product and service offerings, but to enable those clients to achieve a vastly different level of performance themselves.

drugs, now between 5 and 10 percent, to 50 percent or better. IBM also believes that it can help cut the time it takes to identify and launch a new drug to three to five years, down from ten to twelve, slicing the prelaunch cost of drug development to less than $200 million, from $800 million.

It's a splendid vision—and far too rich with opportunity for IBM alone. Microsoft has more cash than any tech company ($43 billion), and its .net Windows initiative is an effort to rule the next generation of computing that's every bit as ambitious as Palmisano's. But Microsoft trails Big Blue in the upper end of the corporate computing world. Sun Microsystems, an early advocate of on-demand computing, is pushing its own effort to develop software, called N1, that will manage Sun gear more efficiently. Sun claims that N1 will offer superior performance—at one-tenth the cost—because the software is designed only for Sun products. "Diversity is great in your workforce," says Sun Executive Vice President Jonathan Schwartz. "It sucks in your data center." IBM software head Steven A. Mills shoots back: "Nothing they have in N1 is unique."

A stronger contender is Hewlett-Packard, thanks to its array of hardware, software, and services. Analysts say that HP leads IBM in a few important niches. HP, for example, has software called Utility Data Center that shifts work across all of a company's computers, networks, and storage devices.

For now, IBM's wide-angle vision and broader range of technology give it the overall lead. But to stay ahead, Palmisano maintains a routine of near-constant work. Even while on a Vermont ski vacation in early March, Palmisano spent a snowy Sunday afternoon reading briefing papers while his family hit the slopes. Rest assured that Palmisano won't be getting his weekends back anytime soon. He is remaking IBM, and that's a job that could last a full decade. If he pulls it off, though, a giant of technology will be reborn.

MONDAY MORNING...

THE PROBLEMS
Revitalizing an ailing technology giant in an
increasingly competitive world

THE SOLUTION
Find a way to harness IBM's unique strengths in both
engineering and customer management to design
a technology platform for the future.

SUSTAINING THE WIN
Create an organization and culture that enable
creativity and collaboration.

YUN JONG YONG:
THE SAMSUNG WAY

Courtesy of Getty Images.

POWER PLAYER
CEO and vice chairman Yun
Jong Yong has led the consumer
electronics conglomerate through
a remarkable turnaround with
a surprisingly unconventional
technology strategy, favoring
hardware and gadgets over
software and content.

This story by Cliff Edwards, Moon Ihlwan, and Pete
Engardio from 2003, with updates from 2006, sets
the agenda for coverage of the Korean giant.

Go from unknown to
ubiquitous without
oversaturating
consumer mindshare.
Turn a low-cost
imitator into an
innovative leader of
the premium
marketplace.

Recover from
enormous write-offs,
unwise acquisitions,
and tremendous
debt.

Become a highly
profitable company,
all the while ignoring
conventional wisdom
and historical
precedent.

LESSON PLAN

PUT PRODUCTS EVERYWHERE

A black-suited Agent Smith sprints down a city street. As he is felled by an acrobatic kung fu kick from Trinity, the camera pulls back to show that the action is taking place inside a giant, floating Samsung TV. The screen rotates, revealing that the set is just three inches thick. "You cannot escape the Samsung 40-inch LCD flat-panel TV," intones the baritone voice of actor Laurence Fishburne. "Welcome to the new dimension."

The ad, now appearing in many U.S. theaters showing *The Matrix: Reloaded*, has an element of truth: whether you're a consumer in America, Europe, or Asia, it's getting pretty darn hard to escape things made by Samsung Electronics Co. Take the United States alone. Stroll the aisles of Best Buy Co. electronics stores, and stylish Samsung high-definition TVs, phones, plasma displays, and digital music and video players are everywhere. Log on to the home pages of *USA Today*, CNN, and other heavily trafficked sites, and Samsung's ads are the first to pop out. You see its blue elliptical logo emblazoned on Olympic scoreboards. And expect more Matrix tie-ins: Samsung is selling a wireless phone just like the one Keanu Reeves uses to transport himself in the movie. Samsung will be even more visible in this fall's sequel, *The Matrix: Revolutions*.

Samsung's *Matrix* moment is the latest step in its reincarnation as one of the world's coolest brands. Its success with a blizzard of digital gadgets and with chips has wowed consumers and scared rivals around the world. The achievement is all the more remarkable considering that just six years ago, Samsung was financially crippled, with its brand having become associated with cheap, me-too TVs and microwaves.

Now the company seems to be entering a new dimension. Its feature-jammed gadgets are racking up design awards, and the company is rapidly muscling its way to the top of consumer brand awareness surveys. Samsung thinks the moment is fast arriving when it can unseat Sony Corp. as the most valuable electronics brand and the most important shaper of digital trends. "We believe we can be number one," says Samsung America Chief Executive Oh Dong Jin. The company's rivals are taking the challenge seriously. "I ask for a report on what Samsung is doing every week," says Sony President Kunitake Ando.

LEAD INNOVATION

Here are a few measures of Samsung's progress: it has become the biggest maker of digital mobile phones using code-division multiple access technology—and while it still lags behind number two, Motorola Inc., in handsets sold, it has just passed it in overall global revenues. A year ago, you'd have been hard pressed to find a Samsung high-definition TV in the United States. Now, Samsung is the best-selling brand in TVs priced at $3,000 and above—a mantle long held by Sony and Mitsubishi Corp. In the new market for digital music players, Samsung's three-year-old Yepp is behind only the Rio of Japan's D&M Holdings Inc. and Apple Computer Inc.'s iPod. Samsung has blown past Micron Technology, Infineon Technologies, and Hynix Semiconductor in dynamic random-access memory (DRAM) chips (used in all PCs) and is gaining on Intel in flash memory, used in digital cameras, music players, and handsets. In 2002, with most of techdom reeling, Samsung earned $5.9 billion on sales of $33.8 billion.

POWER MOVE

Samsung's marketing tactics reinforce its product strategy. It's not enough for Samsung to offer the most reliable gadgets or the widest range of features. To compete with Apple, Sony, and Philips, Yun has to make over its brand—a task that will cost hundreds of millions of dollars but position the company in the right league.

Can the good times last? That's a serious question, since Samsung is challenging basic new-economy dogma. In high tech, the assumption is that developing proprietary software and content gives you higher margins and a long lead time over rivals. Yet Samsung defiantly refuses to enter the software business. It's wedded to hardware and is betting that it can thrive in a period of relentless deflation for the industry. Rather than outsource manufacturing, the company sinks billions into huge new factories. Instead of bearing down on a few "core competencies," Samsung remains diversified and vertically integrated—Samsung chips and displays go into its own digital products. "If we get out of manufacturing," says CEO and Vice Chairman Yun Jong Yong, "we will lose."

Yet the industrial history of the past two decades suggests that this model does not work in the long run. The problem—as many Japanese, U.S., and European companies learned in the 1980s and 1990s—is that Samsung must keep investing heavily in R&D and new factories across numerous product lines. Samsung has sunk $19 billion over five years into new chip facilities. Rivals can buy similar technologies from other vendors without tying up capital or making long-term commitments. What's more, the life cycle of much hardware is brutally short and subject to relentless commoditization. The average price of a TV set has dropped 30 percent in five years; a DVD player goes for less than a quarter of what it once did. The Chinese keep driving prices ever lower, leveraging supercheap wages and engineering talent. Meanwhile, the Japanese are building their own Chinese factories to lower their costs. No wonder Samsung exited the low-margin market for TV sets 27 inches and under.

Faced with these perils, Samsung needs a constant stream of well-timed hits to stay on top. Even Sony has stumbled in this race; it now depends on PlayStation to support a consumer-electronics business whose glory days seem to be behind it. Other legendary hardware makers—Apple, Motorola, Ericsson—have learned the perils of the hardware way.

KEEP THE HITS COMING

Investors got a sharp reminder of the risks Samsung is running when the company announced its first-quarter results. In a tough environment, Samsung racked up the biggest market-share gain of any company in handsets, going from 9.3 to 10.5 percent. Yet it had to lower its prices to get there, and lower memory-chip prices also hit the bottom line. The result was a drop in first-quarter profits of 41 percent, to $942 million, on sales of $8 billion. Second-quarter profits could drop further, analysts say, hurt by lower sales in Korea's slumping economy—and in China and other Asian countries struck by the SARS epidemic. Controversy also flared in May when Samsung Electronics agreed to invest a further $93 million in a troubled credit card affiliate. Many critics believe that Samsung should divest the unit but that it is propping it up as both are controlled by the same family. Concern over corporate governance is the big reason that Samsung continues to trade at a discount to its global peers. Even though it's regarded as one of the most transparent emerging-market companies anywhere, Korea's history of corporate scandals means that many foreigners will always suspect its numbers.

If the earnings continue to soften, plenty of investors around the world will stand to lose. Samsung is the most widely held emerging-market stock, with $41 billion in market capitalization, and foreigners hold more than half its shares. Over the past five years, the shares have risen more than tenfold, to a recent $273. But concerns over 2003's earnings have driven the shares off their recent high this year.

The challenges are huge, but so are Samsung's strengths. It is used to big swings: nearly half its profits come from memory chips, a notoriously cyclical business. Even in the weak first quarter, Samsung earned more than any U.S. technology company other than Microsoft, IBM, and Cisco. Meanwhile, Sony lost $940 million in this year's first three months, and chip rivals Micron, Infineon, and Hynix lost a combined $1.88 billion. In cell phones, Samsung has kept its average selling price at $191, compared with $154 for Nokia and $147 for Motorola, according to Technology Business Research. What's more, since 1997, its debt has shrunk from an unsustainable $10.8 billion to $1.4 billion, leaving Samsung in a healthy net cash position. And its net margins have risen from 0.4 percent to 12 percent.

SPEED AND INTELLIGENCE

Driving this success is CEO Yun, a career company man who took over in the dark days of 1997. Yun and his boss, Samsung Group Chairman Lee Kun Hee, recognized that the electronics industry's shift from analog to digital, making many technologies accessible, would leave industry leadership up for grabs. "In the analog era, it was difficult for a latecomer to catch up," Yun says. But in the digital era, "if you are two months late, you're dead. So speed and intelligence are what matter, and the winners haven't yet been determined."

Samsung's strategy to win is pretty basic, but Yun is executing it with ferocious drive over a remarkably broad conglomerate. To streamline, Yun cut 24,000 workers and sold $2 billion in noncore businesses when he took over.

Samsung managers who have worked for big competitors say that they go through far fewer layers of bureaucracy to win approval for new products, budgets, and marketing plans, speeding up their ability to seize opportunities. In a recent speech, Sony Chairman Nobuyuki Idei noted Samsung's "aggressive restructuring" and said: "To survive as a global player, we too have to change."

Second, Samsung often forces its own units to compete with outsiders to get the best solution. In the liquid-crystal-display business, Samsung buys half of its color filters from Sumitomo

Chemical Co. of Japan and sources the other half internally, pitting the two teams against each other. "They really press these departments to compete," says Sumitomo President Hiromasa Yonekura.

The next step is to customize as much as possible. Even in memory chips, the ultimate commodity, Samsung commands prices that are 17 percent above the industry average. A key reason is that 60 percent of its memory devices are custom-made for products like Dell servers, Microsoft Xbox game consoles, and even Nokia's cell phones. "Samsung is one of a handful of companies you can count on to bridge the technical and consumer experiences and bring them successfully to market," says Will Poole, Senior Vice President at Microsoft's Windows Client Business, which works with the Koreans.

POWER MOVE

Today, consumers place a premium on both customization and speed—elements of Samsung's strategy that often seem to be at cross purposes. Though it has risen through the ranks by doing so, Samsung will find it increasingly difficult to improve along both dimensions. Eventually, the company may have to focus on just one.

The final ingredient is speed. Samsung says that it takes an average of 5 months to go from new product concept to rollout, compared to 14 months six years ago. After Samsung persuaded T-Mobile, the German-U.S. cell phone carrier, to market a new camera phone last April, for example, it quickly assembled 80 designers and engineers from its chip, telecom, display, computing, and manufacturing operations. In four months, they had a prototype for the V205, which has an innovative lens that swivels 270 degrees and transmits photos wirelessly. Then Samsung flew 30 engineers to Seattle to field-test the phone on T-Mobile's servers and networks. By November, the phones were rolling out of the Korean plant. Since then, Samsung has sold 300,000 V205s a month at $350 each. Park Sang Jin, executive vice president for mobile communications, estimates that the turnaround time is half what Japanese rivals would require. "Samsung has managed to get all its best companies globally to pull in the same direction, something Toshiba, Motorola, and Sony have faced big challenges in doing," says Allen Delattre, director of Accenture Ltd. high-tech practice.

GLOBAL STRENGTH

Samsung can also use South Korea as a test market. Some 70 percent of the country's homes are wired for broadband, and 20 percent of the population buys a new cell phone every seven months. Samsung already sells a phone in Korea that allows users to download and view up to 30 minutes of video and watch live TV for a fixed monthly fee. Samsung is selling 100,000 video-on-demand phones a month in Korea at $583 each. Verizon plans to introduce them in three U.S. cities this fall.

This year alone, Samsung will launch 95 new products in the United States, including 42 new TVs. Motorola plans to introduce a dozen new cell phone models, says Technology Business Research Inc. analyst Chris Foster. Samsung will launch 20. Nokia also is a whiz at snapping out new models. But most are based on two or three platforms, or basic designs. The 130 models Samsung will introduce globally this year are based on 78 platforms. Whereas Motorola completely changes its product line every 12 to 18 months, Foster says, Samsung refreshes its lineup every 9 months. Samsung has already introduced the first voice-activated phones, handsets with MP3 players, and digital camera phones that send photos over global system for mobile (GSM) communications networks.

Samsung has been just as fast in digital TVs. It became the first to market projection TVs using new chips from Texas Instruments Inc. that employed digital light processing (DLP). DLP chips contain 1.3 million micromirrors that flip at high speeds to create a sharper picture. TI had given Japanese companies the technology early in 1999, but they never figured out how to make the sets economically. Samsung entered the market in late 2001, and already has seven DLP projection sets starting at $3,400 that have become the hottest-selling sets in their price range. "They'll get a product to market a lot faster than their counterparts," says George Danko, Best Buy's senior vice president for consumer electronics.

Samsung hopes that all this is just a warm-up for its bid to dominate the digital home. For years, Philips, Sony, and Apple have been developing home appliances, from handheld computers to intelligent refrigerators, that talk to each other and adapt to consumers' personal needs. Infrastructure bottlenecks and a lack of uniform standards got in the way.

Now, many analysts predict that digital appliances will take off within five years. By then, as many as 40 percent of U.S. households should be wired for high-speed Internet access, and digital TVs, home appliances, and networking devices will be much more affordable. Samsung is showing a version of its networked home in Seoul's Tower Palace apartment complex, where 2,400 families can operate appliances from washing machines to air conditioners by tapping on a wireless "Web pad" device, which doubles as a portable flat-screen TV.

It's a grandiose dream. But if the digital home becomes a reality, Samsung has a chance. "They've got the products, a growing reputation as the innovator, and production lines to back that up," says In-Stat/MDR consumer-electronics analyst Cindy Wolf. With nearly $7 billion in cash, Samsung has plenty to spend on R&D, factories, and marketing.

TOUGH LOVE

Samsung Electronics's ascent is an unlikely tale. The company was left with huge debt following the 1997 Korean financial crisis, a crash in memory-chip prices, and a $700 million write-off after an ill-advised takeover of AST Technologies, a U.S. maker of PCs. Its subsidiaries paid little heed to profits and focused on breaking production and sales records—even if much of the output ended up sitting unsold in warehouses.

A jovial toastmaster at company dinners but a tough-as-nails boss when he wants results, Yun shuttered Samsung's TV factories for two months until old inventory cleared. Yun also decreed that Samsung would sell only high-end goods. Many cellular operators resisted. "Carriers didn't buy our story," says telecom executive Park. "They wanted lower prices all the time. At some point, we had to say no to them."

A top priority was straightening out the business in the United States, where "we were in a desperate position," recalls Samsung America chief Oh, appointed in early 2001. "We had a lot of gadgets. But they had nowhere to go." Samsung lured Peter Skaryznski from AT&T to run handset sales and Peter Weedfald, who worked at ViewSonic Corp. and *ComputerWorld* magazine, to head marketing.

Yun brought new blood to Seoul, too. One recruit was Eric B. Kim, 48, who had moved to the United States from Korea at age 13 and worked at various tech companies. Kim was named executive vice president of global marketing in 1999. With his Korean rusty, Kim made his first big presentation to 400 managers in English. Sensing that Kim would be resented, Yun declared: "Some of you may want to put Mr. Kim on top of a tree and then shake him down. If anybody tries that, I will kill you!"

The first coup in the United States came in 1997, when Sprint PCS Group began selling Samsung handsets. Sprint's service was based on CDMA, and Samsung had an early lead in the standard as a result of an alliance in Korea with Qualcomm Inc. Samsung's SCH-3500, a silver, clamshell-shaped model priced at $149, was an instant hit. Soon, Samsung was the world leader in CDMA phones. Under Weedfald, Samsung also pulled its appliances off the shelves of Wal-Mart and Target and negotiated deals with higher-end chains like Best Buy and Circuit City.

Samsung's status in chips and displays, which can make up 90 percent of the cost of most digital devices, gives it an edge in handsets and other products. Besides dominating DRAM chips, Samsung leads in static random-access memory and controls 55 percent of the $2 billion market for NAND flash memory, a technology that is mainly used in removable cards that store large music and color-image files. With portable digital appliances expected to skyrocket, analysts predict that NAND flash sales will soar to $7 billion by 2005, overtaking the more established market for NOR flash, which is embedded into PCs and is dominated by Intel and Advanced Micro Devices.

The company's breadth in displays gives it a similar advantage. It leads in thin-film LCDs, which are becoming the favored format for PCs, normal-size TVs, and all mobile devices. Samsung predicts that a factory being built in Tangjung, Korea, that will produce LCD sheets as big as a queen-size mattress will help to halve prices of large-screen LCD TVs by 2005. Samsung also aims to be number one in plasma and projection displays.

USE PARTNERSHIPS STRATEGICALLY

If Samsung has a major flaw, it may be its lack of software and content. Samsung has no plans to branch out into music, movies, and games, as Sony and Apple have done. Sony figures that subscriptions to content will provide a more lucrative source of revenue. Samsung's executives remain convinced that they're better off collaborating with content and software providers. They say that this strategy offers customers more choices than Nokia, which uses its own software.

Yun has heard tech gurus, publications, and even Samsung executives warn him to forsake the vertical model. His response: Samsung needs it all. "Everyone can get the same technology now," he says. "But that doesn't mean they can make an advanced product." Stay at the forefront of core technologies and master the manufacturing, Yun believes, and you control your future. Many technology companies have tried that strategy and failed. Samsung is betting billions that it can overcome the odds.

POWER MOVE

To be sure, Samsung has thrived so far by defying conventional wisdom. But as globalization marches on, other former low-cost imitators in emerging markets—especially China and India—are increasing in speed and sophistication themselves. Yun needs to keep his eye on his steadily approaching competitors. A newer, nimbler version of Samsung could be just over the horizon.

SAMSUNG'S HIGH-DESIGN, LOWER-PROFIT CELL PHONE STRATEGY

You can count on Samsung Electronics executives to put a brave face on it when they announce their smallest quarterly operating profit in nearly three years on July 14.

Analysts expect Samsung to report operating profits of about $1.35 billion in the three months ending in June. That's a better earnings performance than key global rivals, but it underscores the problems the South Korean national champion is having in two critical markets: flash memory chips and liquid-crystal panels. Samsung executives concede as much, although they think the earnings stall is pretty much over.

"We are doing okay," says Samsung Senior Vice President Chu Woo Sik. "We've gone past the bottom, and the second half looks much brighter."

Samsung, of course, is still a killer innovator and the most profitable information technology player in Asia. And Samsung investors can take some comfort in the fact that rival LG. Philips LCD, a key competitor in the liquid-crystal display panel business, recently posted a record quarterly net loss of $340 million [see BusinessWeek.com, 7/11/06, LG. Philips LCD Swings to Loss in 2Q].

WATCH MARKET SHIFTS

Samsung is still making money from its LCD unit, thanks to its focus on hot-selling big flat-screen TVs. The profit margin from flash chips, used for MP3 music players, digital cameras, and other mobile gadgets, will be just below 30 percent, far below the approximately 40 percent of the end of last year. That's not sensational, but it's hardly a disaster, either.

The far bigger worry is Samsung's slide in the global mobile phone arena, which used to be a money-spinner. Two years ago, Samsung looked as if it had a shot at displacing Motorola as the world's number two handset maker, just after Nokia. Now, the Korean company is a distant number three, and analysts don't expect it to catch up to Motorola anytime soon.

The reason: Samsung is missing in action in critical emerging markets for the fast-growing low-end handsets, such as India. Since the late 1990s, Samsung has tried to establish itself as a high-end player and an ultra-cool brand by focusing on stylish, feature-packed products. The plan worked, but the company seems to have missed the big market shift to less expensive phones in recent years. "Samsung is a victim of its own success," says technology analyst Daniel Kim at Merrill Lynch in Seoul.

CONSTANT REINVENTION

The focus on high-end products allowed hard-charging Samsung to emerge out of nowhere as a trend setter. In the past several years, it has led a switch to color from black-and-white screens, and it became the first to make phones that doubled as MP3 players and mobile TVs. It also popularized the clamshell design and kept rolling out camera phones with increasingly high resolution.

The gambit is no longer working. With the cell phone market in the developed world saturated, the big growth is coming in emerging markets, where first-time users still abound. "I like Samsung because of the speed with which it responds to changing business environments, but when it comes to phones, the company still lives in the old paradigm," says Ahn Young Hoe, chief investment officer at fund manager KTB Asset Management in Seoul. "It certainly risks diminishing market share."

Already there are signs that Samsung is losing out. The consensus among analysts is that in the second quarter of this year, Samsung won't be able to match its first-quarter sales of 29 million phones. Worse, its profit margin is set to slip back from 10 percent in January to March of this year to closer to the 8 percent it posted in the fourth quarter of last year. Compare this to its margin of 17 percent a year earlier.

FOCUS ON THE PREMIUM

Samsung maintains that it is not neglecting the entry-level markets. However, "our priority is in maintaining our brand image as a maker of premium products with leading-edge technologies," says Executive Vice President Kim Woon Sub, a key figure for charting Samsung's business strategy. "Our basic business approach is clear: we won't compromise profits for the sake of a bigger market share. Even in the entry markets, our focus will be the premium segment."

Executives argue that Samsung should be able to keep its standing in the industry without competing with Nokia or Motorola for phones costing $50 or less. In the first quarter of this year, for example, Samsung's phone unit sales rose 18 percent from a year earlier, they point out. The trouble is, rivals' sales grew at a much faster pace. Nokia's sales jumped 40 percent, to 75.1 million phones, during the period and Motorola's 61 percent, to 46.1 million.

A bigger problem lies in profitability. Although Samsung limited its marketing efforts largely to mid- to high-end phones, its operational income dropped 45 percent, to $486 million, in the first three months of this year. In contrast, Nokia and Motorola posted income increases of 32 percent, to $1.34 billion, and 60 percent, to $702 million, respectively, in the period.

The numbers underscore the need for the Korean company to lower its costs. One way to do so could be to outsource manufacturing and globalize the sources of components to include suppliers in Taiwan, China, and India, where costs are lower than in Korea. Yet a spokeswoman at Samsung says that her company has no plans to outsource the production of

POWER MOVE

Recent years have seen scores of high-end designers move successfully to the masses. Isaac Mizrahi housewares have scored points with shoppers at Target, and at major metropolitan locations of the trendy international clothing retailer H&M, Stella McCartney's affordable line sold out in hours. Samsung is brave to stick to its guns, but there might be yet another option.

phones for the sake of cutting costs because that would make it hard for the company to control quality.

Instead, Samsung's answer is to roll out a profusion of fancy new models that executives hope will drive both sales and earnings. Last month, it unveiled three ultra-thin phones to tap the runaway success of Motorola's thin clamshell RAZR.

"The biggest differentiating factor these days is design," Chu said, noting that mobile carriers have been slow to migrate to next-generation networks .

FOCUS ON FEATURES

In an attempt to beat its U.S. rival in its own going-slim game, Samsung last month in Europe started selling the X820 model, which is just 6.9 mm thick, compared with 14 mm for RAZR. The bar-shaped phone sports a two-megapixel camera and a case of fiberglass-infused plastic.

This month it is launching in Asia and Europe the clamshell D830, with a 9.9-mm-thick magnesium body, and the D900 slider phone, which is 12.9 mm thick. Joining them in Europe is a new slim smartphone with a QWERTY keypad, the SGH-i320, to compete with Motorola's. Samsung is negotiating with a U.S. carrier to bring all these phones here soon.

Samsung hopes that its focus on handsets with cutting-edge features such as 3.5-G services and mobile TV will eventually pay off. London-based researcher Informa Telecoms & Media forecasts that the TV broadcasting market could be worth $8.4 billion by 2010.

"We are well placed to take the lead once mobile television and high-speed wireless Internet service become widespread," says Chu. Maybe, but Samsung will first have to make sure it won't be outgunned by its rivals because it missed the boom in low-end handsets for emerging markets.

MONDAY MORNING...

THE PROBLEM
Staying ahead of low-cost competitors who can—
and will—copy your moves in a millisecond

Increasing profits without relying on high-margin
products

THE SOLUTION
Capture the premium market with rapid innovation
and disciplined execution.

Establish your brand to match your products:
prestigious, sleek, and fast.

SUSTAINING THE WIN
Use your home market to test risky, innovative
offerings, but study the differences in consumer
behavior among populations carefully.

ARTHUR J. SULZBERGER: THE NEW YORK TIMES AND THE FUTURE OF NEWSPAPERS

POWER PLAYER

Arthur Sulzberger Jr., heir to the New York Times Co., faces dwindling circulation and defecting advertisers and the viability of the traditional newspaper business model. His hands are full as he deals with weaker earnings, a changing media world, and a scandal's aftermath.

This 2005 cover story by Anthony Bianco with John Rossant and Lauren Gard examines Sulzberger's strategy to deliver top-notch journalism in any form, any place.

Regain the public's trust after a scandal that damaged the company's credibility.

Develop a strategy that satisfies digital-age consumers but doesn't sacrifice the company's journalistic integrity.

LESSON PLAN

REGAIN CREDIBILITY

Since 1896, four generations of the Ochs-Sulzberger family have guided the *New York Times* through wars, recessions, strikes, and innumerable family crises. In 2003, though, Arthur Ochs Sulzberger Jr., the current proprietor, faced what seemed to be a publisher's ultimate test after a loosely supervised young reporter named Jayson Blair was found to have fabricated dozens of stories. The revelations sparked a newsroom rebellion that humiliated Sulzberger, forcing him to fire Executive Editor Howell Raines. "My heart is breaking," Sulzberger admitted to his staff on the day he showed Raines the door.

It turns out, though, that fate was not finished with Sulzberger, who is also chairman of the newspaper's corporate parent, New York Times Co.—The strife that convulsed the *New York Times*'s newsroom under the tyrannical Raines has faded under the measured leadership of his successor, Bill Keller, but now the paper's financial performance is lagging. NYT Co.'s stock is trading at about 40, down 25 percent from its high of 53.80 in mid-2002, and has trailed the shares of many other newspaper companies for a good year and a half. "Their numbers in this recovery are bordering on the abysmal," says Douglas Arthur, Morgan Stanley's senior publishing analyst.

Meanwhile, the once-Olympian authority of the *Times* is being eroded not only by its own journalistic screw-ups (from the Blair scandal to erroneous reports of weapons of mass destruction in Iraq), but also by profound changes in communications technology and in the U.S. political climate. There are those who contend that the newspaper has been permanently diminished, as has the rest of what now is dismissively known in some circles as "MSM," or mainstream media. "The Roman Empire that was mass media is breaking up, and we are entering an almost-feudal period where there will be many more centers of power and influence," maintains Orville Schell, dean of the University of California at Berkeley's journalism school. "It's a kind of disaggregation of the molecular structure of the media."

The pride that Sulzberger takes in his journalistic legacy is palpable, and his knowledge of the *Times*'s august history, encyclopedic. Yet "Young Arthur," as he is still known to some at age

53, exudes a wisecracking, live-wire vitality more typical of a founding entrepreneur than of an heir. He began an interview for this article by picking up a big hunk of metal from a conference room table and brandishing it menacingly. "Ask any question you'd like," he growled and then deposited the object in a less obtrusive spot. "It's an award," he added softly.

A NEW BUSINESS MODEL

Sulzberger, who succeeded his father as publisher in 1992 and as chairman in 1997, has already rescued the *New York Times* from decline once. With the help of then-CEO Russell T. Lewis, he reinvented the "Gray Lady" by devising a radical solution to the threat of eroding circulation that had imperiled the *Times* and other big-city dailies for years. Sulzberger changed the paper itself by spending big money to add new sections and a profusion of color illustration. At the same time, he made the *Times* the first—and still the only—metro newspaper in America to broaden its distribution beyond its home city to encompass the entire country. Today, nearly 50 percent of all subscribers to the weekday *Times* live somewhere other than Gotham.

The Sulzbergers who preceded him were newspapermen; Arthur Jr., by his own description, is a "platform-agnostic" multimedia man. In the mid-1990s, NYT Co. became one of the first Old Media companies to move into cyberspace. *Times* reporters also began experimenting with adapting their newspaper stories to another medium that was new to them—television. Today, NYTimes.com consistently ranks among the 10 most popular Internet news sites, and New York Times Television is one of the largest independent producers of documentary programming in the United States. "Within our lifetimes, the distribution of news and information is going to shift to broadband," Sulzberger says. "We must enter the broadband world

POWER MOVE

The jury is still out as to whether distributing the Times around the country will pay off. True, its ubiquity helps to position it as the country's leading news organization. But, with the dramatic growth in online news consumption, perhaps it should be strengthening its presence in alternative channels, such as audio files and wireless phone alerts.

having mastered the three key skill sets—print, Internet, and video—because that's what's going to ensure the future of this news organization in the years ahead."

Sulzberger acknowledges that he and his company are embattled in the present: "These are tough times, and they've been tough times for a while." But he and new CEO Janet L. Robinson (Lewis retired at the end of 2004) are sticking with the long-term plan set nearly a decade ago: enhancing the content of the *Times* and extending its reach into virgin territories west of the Hudson, while also building its multimedia capacity. In 2002, NYT Co. added a global dimension to its growth strategy by acquiring full control of the *International Herald Tribune*, which is now being upgraded and expanded.

QUALITY PAYS

In essence, Sulzberger is doing what his forebears have always done: sink money into the *Times* in the belief that quality journalism pays in the long run. "The challenge is to remember that our history is to invest during tough times," he says. "And when those times turn—and they do, inevitably—we will be well positioned for recovery."

Will it work this time? Will toughing it out Sulzberger-style revitalize the *Times* or consign it to creeping irrelevance? "Despite all that has happened, I still think that the *New York Times* has a stature and a position of journalistic authority that is greater than any news organization in the world. Could that be destroyed? I believe that it could be," says Alex S. Jones, a former *Times* media critic who is coauthor of *The Trust*, a history of the Sulzbergers and their newspaper. Jones, who now runs the Joan Shorenstein Center on the Press, Politics & Public Policy at Harvard University, hastens to add that he hopes that the paper will thrive again. "I tell you, I hate to think of it not succeeding," he says.

The constancy of their commitment to high-cost journalism has put the Sulzbergers in an increasingly contrarian position. Many of the country's surviving big-city dailies once were owned by similarly high-minded dynastic families, but those families long ago surrendered control to big public corporations that prize earnings per share above all else. Editorial budgets at most newspapers, as well as at TV and radio stations, have been squeezed so hard for so long that asphyxiation is a mounting risk. The proliferation of Web sites and cable-TV stations has produced an abundance of commentary and analysis, but the kind of thorough, original reporting in which the *Times* specializes is, if anything, increasingly scarce.

In effect, the Sulzbergers have subsidized the *Times* in valuing good journalism and the prestige it confers over profits and the wealth they create. In fact, for much of its history, the *Times* barely broke even. Recasting the paper into a publicly held corporation capable of pursuing profit as determinedly as *Times* editors chase Pulitzers was the signal achievement of Arthur Jr.'s father, Arthur O. "Punch" Sulzberger Sr. Still, NYT Co. consistently fails to post the 25 percent profit margins of such big newspaper combines as Gannett Co. and Knight-Ridder Inc. mainly because of the *Times*'s outsize editorial spending, which the paper does not disclose but which is thought to exceed $300 million a year.

For a time, Arthur Jr. enthralled Wall Street by adding double-digit growth to the Sulzbergian formula. The value of NYT Co. shares soared 295 percent from their 1996 low to their 2002 high, boosting the value of the family's 19 percent holding to $1.5 billion. Like other Old Media families, the Sulzbergers have been able to maintain unquestioned control of their company by creating a second class of voting stock and reserving most of it for themselves. Among them, the various branches of the Sulzberger family control 91 percent of the Class B voting shares.

The Bancrofts of Dow Jones & Co. and the Grahams of Washington Post Co. share the Sulzbergers' journalism-first philosophy. However, Washington Post Co. has moved beyond newspapering to a greater extent than has NYT Co., which in addition to the *Herald Tribune* owns the *Boston Globe*, 15 small daily newspapers, and eight television stations. Actually, Arthur Jr. has increased his company's financial reliance on the *Times* by selling off magazines and other peripheral properties acquired under his father. In short, NYT Co. is quality journalism's purest traditional play.

In 2004, the company clearly failed to parlay quality into the growth it will need to continue supporting the *Times* franchise. The Wall Street consensus is that the company will report net income of $290 million for 2004, down 4 percent from the preceding year and a good 35 percent below the $445 million it netted in the media industry boom year of 2001. In 2005, revenues plateaued at $3 billion, give or take a few hundred million.

WHEN CHANGE BREEDS SCANDAL

It wasn't that long ago—April 8, 2002, to be precise—that all seemed right in Arthur Sulzberger Jr.'s rarified world. On that day, most of the *Times*'s 1,200 reporters and editors gathered in its newsroom just off Times Square to celebrate the paper's record haul of Pulitzer Prizes. No newspaper had ever before won more than four Pulitzers in a year; in 2002, the *Times* won seven—six of which recognized its Herculean coverage of the September 11 terrorist attacks and their aftermath. Sulzberger was ecstatic, not realizing that he already had made the biggest blunder of his tenure as publisher: naming Howell Raines as executive editor.

Raines, who had joined the paper in 1978 as a national correspondent, had deeply impressed Sulzberger by shaking the stodginess out of the editorial page as its editor during the Clinton years. Raines campaigned hard for the promotion in 2001, vowing to root out complacency and do whatever was needed to raise the staff's "competitive metabolism." By most accounts, Sulzberger saw Raines, then 58, as his journalistic alter ego and collaborator in transforming the *Times* into a fully national, multimedia franchise.

Just 18 months after self-proclaimed "change agent" Raines had taken charge, the *Times* ran a devastatingly self-critical article recounting how Jayson Blair had plagiarized or made up at least 36 stories. Sulzberger, who has often been accused of lacking gravitas, will be a long time living down his flip initial reaction to Blair's transgressions: "It sucks." Worse, Sulzberger had no feel for how Raines was perceived in the newsroom, where resentment of his arbitrary, self-aggrandizing ways had reached the flash point. Three weeks after Sulzberger had unequivocally affirmed his support for Raines, the publisher fired him and Managing Editor Gerald Boyd.

PAY ATTENTION TO WHAT'S GOING ON INSIDE

The Blair-Raines fiasco devastated Sulzberger. But after a long period of introspection, he appears to have regained his confidence, if not quite his swagger. "There's no question that the experience changed him," says Steven L. Rattner, a prominent private equity investor who has been one of Sulzberger's closest confidants ever since they worked together as young *Times* reporters in the late 1970s. "It's made him more open to other views and more careful to have a better sense of what's going on," he says. "I think it has been an eye-opening experience for Arthur, and that's never bad for any of us."

Sulzberger swallowed a heaping helping of humble pie in replacing Raines with Keller, a former managing editor whom he had passed over in promoting Raines. Appointed in July 2003, Keller, 54, has been editor for only as long as Raines was, but already has made a number of changes as fundamental as those that his predecessor promulgated yet never implemented. "I cringed every time I read that people thought my job was to come in and calm the place down because it made me sound like the official dispenser of Zoloft," says Keller, whose gracious manner has often been mistaken for passivity. "I saw myself instead as being, in some sense, a change agent without having to wave a revolutionary banner."

Keller has made so many high-level personnel changes that two-thirds of all newsroom workers now report to a new boss. He has also put into practice a string of reforms suggested by several internal committees formed in the wake of the Blair affair. These include the appointment of a standards editor and a public editor, or ombudsman. By most accounts, the *Times* now is much more responsive to outside complaints and criticism than it was.

INNOVATE BECAUSE YOUR CUSTOMERS DEMAND IT

At considerable expense, the paper also has redesigned a half-dozen of its sections and upgraded its global culture coverage with the addition of 20 writing and editing jobs. "In the last year, there has been more change in a packed period of time than I've seen at this paper ever," says Sulzberger, who also credits Keller with "steadying our culture and lowering the temperature here." It is no mean feat to simultaneously improve morale and shake things up, but Keller is going to have to make certain that a happier newsroom does not again make for a more complacent newsroom. What Raines derided as "the *Times*'s defining myth of effortless superiority" might now be in remission—but has it been eradicated?

POWER MOVE

At some point, even the most fiercely independent company has to answer to its audience. First, the public deserves that measure of respect from the Times—and from all other news organizations. And, as bloggers and smaller, independent news sources gain traction in the battle for mind share, the public can demand it.

While the *Times* appears to be regaining its stride journalistically, it has not been rewarded with circulation gains. In 2004, the paper posted an infinitesimal 0.2 percent increase in the circulation of both the daily edition, which now stands at about 1.1 million, and the Sunday paper, which is just under 1.7 million. Since the national expansion began in 1998, the *Times* has added 150,000 daily subscribers outside New York but is thought to have lost about 96,000 subscribers in its home market. However, the net increase of 54,000 represents a 5.1 percent uptick, which compares with the 3.5 percent decline in U.S. daily newspaper circulation over this period. What's more, the *Times* posted its gains despite boosting the price of a subscription by more than 25 percent on average.

New subscribers are increasingly hard to come by for all newspapers as advances in digital communications spur the proliferation of alternative sources of news and information. For the under-30 set in particular, digital accessibility and interactivity tend to trump the familiarity of long-established names like the *New York Times*, CBS, or CNN.

POLITICAL CHALLENGES

The growing polarization of the body politic along ideological lines also is hurting the *Times* and its big-media brethren. One of the few things on which Bush and Kerry supporters agreed during the presidential campaign was that the press was unfair in its coverage of their candidate. Keller says the *Times* was deluged with "ferocious letters berating us for either being stooges of the Bush Administration or agents of Michael Moore." Complaints from the Right were far more numerous, even before the newspaper painted a bull's-eye on itself by running a column by public editor Daniel Okrent headlined "Is *The New York Times* a Liberal Newspaper?" Okrent's short answer: "Of course it is."

What a growing, or at least an increasingly strident, segment of the population seems to want is not journalism untainted by the personal views of journalists, but coverage that affirms their partisan beliefs—in the way that many Fox News shows cater to a conservative constituency. For years, major news organizations have been accused of falling short of the ideal of impartiality that they espouse. Now, the very notion of impartiality is under assault, blurring the line between journalism and propaganda.

For its part, the Bush White House has succeeded to a degree in marginalizing the national or "elite" press by limiting public access to much of the workings of the government and by treating the Fourth Estate as merely another special-interest group that can be safely ignored when it isn't being exploited. The Bushies particularly dislike the *Times*, which, in their view, epitomizes the Eastern liberal Establishment. In his acceptance speech at the Republican convention, George W. Bush mocked the *Times* for what he considered its overly pessimistic coverage of post-World War II Germany. "Maybe that same person is still around, writing editorials," he joked.

The *Times* also is under attack from another branch of the federal government—the judiciary. The paper figures centrally in most of a half-dozen pending court cases that collectively pose a dire threat to the traditional journalistic practice of assuring confidentiality to whistle-blowers and other informants. A federal judge ordered Judith Miller of the *Times* imprisoned for up to 18 months for refusing to testify before a grand jury investigating the leaking of the identity of CIA operative Valerie Plame to conservative columnist Robert Novak. Miller, who researched the Plame affair but never wrote about it.

Sulzberger, who spent six years as a reporter, is outraged that journalists are being slapped with contempt charges for refusing to yield confidential sources to prosecutors. "Reporters are going to jail for doing their jobs, and that's just wrong," he says. The publisher has been less outspoken in responding to the paper's political assailants. In an interview with *BusinessWeek*, though, he denied that his paper is biased in its coverage of national politics or the war in Iraq, or even that it is liberal. The term he prefers is "urban," says Sulzberger. "What we saw play out in this election was urban vs. suburban-rural, not red state vs. blue state," he says. "We are from an urban environment; it comes with the territory. We recognize that, and we can't walk away from it, but neither can we play it politically. I don't think we do."

For the first time since he became publisher, Sulzberger must carry on without Russ Lewis at his side. Lewis, a loquacious lawyer who got his start as a *Times* copy boy in 1966, stepped down after seven years as president and CEO of NYT Co. His replacement is the 54-year-old Janet Robinson, a former schoolteacher who joined the company in 1983 and worked her way up through advertising sales. She played an important role in the national expansion of the

Times as its president and general manager from 1996 into 2004. On the Street, Robinson is known as a formidable manager who relentlessly puts NYT Co.'s best foot forward. "She's never met a number she couldn't spin positively," one analyst says.

WHEN ADVERTISING DECLINES

The most pressing business problem the new CEO faces is a paucity of advertising. Through November, the *Times*'s ad revenues were just 2.3 percent ahead of the previous year—a surprisingly weak performance, considering that the newspaper industry as a whole reported a 9.7 percent gain in national advertising revenues during the first nine months, according to TNS Media Intelligence/CMR. Expenditures on local newspaper advertising in the industry rose 6.6 percent.

A strengthening U.S. economy would help the *Times* in 2005 but wouldn't necessarily restore it to competitive parity. The huge runup in advertising rates over the last decade is forcing more U.S. companies to economize, either by shifting into lower-cost media or by homing in more precisely on their target markets. Neither trend bodes well for the *Times*, whose unique status as America's only metro daily with national reach appears to be putting it at a tactical disadvantage in some ways.

The *Times* has many fewer readers outside of New York City than do the two largest national newspapers—*USA Today* and the *Wall Street Journal,* both of which have circulations far in excess of 2 million. "Those two papers tend to be a more cost-effective buy than the *Times* just because their circulation across the country is so much larger," says Jeff Piper, vice president and general manager of Carat Press, a big media buyer. Even in the New York region, where the *Times* reaches only 14 percent of all adult readers, the paper's circulation is too diffuse to allow for effective targeting by ZIP code—a technique that has enriched many other metro dailies with revenue from inserts.

Robinson maintains that there is nothing wrong with the *Times*'s market position that a growing national and New York economy can't fix. Underscoring her confidence, the paper just imposed what is now an annual January 1 ad rate increase, layering a 5 percent hike atop a cumulative 38 percent increase since 2000. "We feel that premium quality equals premium price," Robinson says.

AGGRESSIVE PRICING

At the same time, the *Times* continues to move out from the 312 markets in which the paper is available into adjacent precincts. In October 2004, it began printing the national edition in Dayton, Ohio, in a plant owned by the local daily. That enabled it to sell papers in 100 new ZIP codes while raising its presence in existing markets as far afield as Louisville. It plans to add seven new contract sites to its network of 20 printing plants by the end of 2006.

POWER MOVE

Price increases do more than boost revenues. They also serve to signal an aggressive strategy to the marketplace. Customers know that they are paying for a premium product, and competitors know that a price war will only destroy value.

The reinvention of the *Times* as a national paper has been accompanied by a steady loss of subscribers in the New York metro area. Its dwindling presence at home has been caused in part by forces beyond its control, including a big influx of non-English-speaking immigrants. However, taking the paper further upscale in pursuit of an elite nationwide readership priced it out of some New Yorkers' reach (a seven-day subscription goes for about $480 a year) and constrained its spending on local marketing and promotion. In addition, the *Times* has declined to join in the trend of introducing foreign-language editions or free editions for young adult readers. (It may be rethinking its free-paper aversion, as evidenced by the *Boston Globe*'s recent purchase of a 49 percent stake in *Metro Boston*, a giveaway tabloid.)

The substitution of national for local subscribers has benefited the *Times* financially even beyond the sizable premium it earns on national advertising. On average, it costs the *Times* about one-third more to produce and deliver a newspaper in its home market (the only place where it owns its printing plants) than in the rest of America. But Sulzberger bristles at the notion that the *Times* is writing off its hometown readers or that a declining New York circulation is the inevitable result of national expansion. "We are not walking away from New York," he says. "But we are growing elsewhere."

The sphere of NYT Co.'s ambitions widened to encompass the globe when it muscled Washington Post Co. aside to gain full control of the *International Herald Tribune*, America's broadsheet voice abroad since 1887. The *Post* reluctantly agreed to relinquish its 50 percent interest for $65 million after NYT Co. threatened to start a new paper to drive the *IHT* out of business. "The thing was going sideways and sooner or later was going to die," says Sulzberger, who was harshly criticized by some for lacking the gentlemanliness of his father.

GO GLOBAL, STAY LOCAL

The company considered making the *Tribune* over into a foreign edition of the *Times*, but decided in the end to maintain *IHT*'s separate, international identity. "This needs to be a European paper for Europeans," says Michael Golden, a NYT Co. vice chairman who was named publisher of *IHT* in 2003. Actually, the *Trib*'s 240,000 subscribers are concentrated in Europe but spread among 180 countries.

POWER MOVE

The separation between the two papers will pay off. IHT will inherit the gravitas, prestige, and journalistic integrity of the Times, but will remain independent enough to maintain its objectivity. As a truly international newspaper, the IHT will attract a much larger audience.

Under Golden, a slightly older first cousin of Sulzberger's, the *Trib* has adopted the *Times*'s playbook, if not its name. The transatlantic flow of copy from the *Times* has increased, but the *Trib* has enlarged its own news staff, too. It has also added pages, color photos, and new printing sites in Sydney, São Paulo, and Kuwait City. The *Trib* scored impressively in recent reader surveys in Europe and Asia, and ad sales are rising, but they still amount to less than $100 million a year. Golden and his cousin yearn to turn the *Trib*'s operating losses into profits, but the general track record of English-language newspapers and magazines abroad is discouraging. Even if the *IHT* flourishes, it will be a long time before it contributes significantly to its parent company's top or bottom line.

The same is true of NYT Co.'s investment in television news. The *Times* has built a cadre of television professionals who, in collaboration with a revolving cast of print reporters, have produced much fine work for *Frontline*, *Nova*, and other programs. In 2003, the *Times* moved beyond production into distribution, laying out $100 million for half-ownership of a digital cable channel, Discovery Times, operated in partnership with Discovery Communications Inc. Discovery Times reaches 35 million homes—an impressive total for a fledgling channel—but its ratings are minuscule: In October, just 27,000 people tuned in during prime time, according to Nielsen//NetRatings.

DIGITAL STRATEGY

Online, the *Times* already is making serious money. New York Times Digital (which includes Boston.com as well as NYTimes.com) netted an enviable $17.3 million on revenues of $53.1 million during the first half of 2004, the last period for which its financials have been disclosed. All indications are that the digital unit is continuing to grow at 30 to 40 percent a year, making it NYT Co.'s fastest-revving growth engine.

Advertising accounts for almost all of the digital operation's revenues, but disagreement rages within the company over whether NYTimes.com should emulate the *Wall Street Journal* and begin charging a subscription fee. Undoubtedly, many of the site's 18 million unique monthly visitors would flee if they were hit with a $39.95 or even a $9.95 monthly charge. One camp within NYT Co. argues that such a massive loss of Web traffic would cost the *Times* dearly in the long run, both by shrinking the audience for its journalism and by depriving it of untold millions in ad revenue. The counterargument is that the *Times* would more than make up for lost ad dollars by boosting circulation revenue—both from online fees and from new print subscriptions paid for by people who now read for free on the Web.

Sulzberger declines to take a side in this debate, but sounds as if he is leaning toward a pay site. "It gets to the issue of how comfortable we are training a generation of readers to get quality information for free," he says. "That is troubling."

What's a platform agnostic to do? The *New York Times*, like all print publications, faces a quandary. A majority of the paper's

POWER MOVE

In 2005, the Times compromised. It began charging for access to Times Select content: major columnists and up to 100 archive articles each month. By mid-2006, more than 400,000 members were generating about $6 million in sales. With college students and home subscribers receiving discounted and free membership, respectively, and depressing total revenues, the hybrid model still receives mixed reviews.

readership now views the paper online, but the company still derives 90 percent of its revenues from newspapering. "The business model that seems to justify the expense of producing quality journalism is the one that isn't growing, and the one that is growing—the Internet—isn't producing enough revenue to produce journalism of the same quality," says John Battelle, a cofounder of *Wired* and other magazines and Web sites.

Today, Sulzberger faces an even bigger challenge than when he took charge of the *Times* in the mid-1990s. Can he find a way to rekindle growth while preserving the primacy of the *Times*'s journalism? The answer will go a long way toward determining not only the fate of America's most important newspaper, but also whether traditional, reporting-intensive journalism has a central place in the Digital Age.

THE PROBLEM
Leading the family business—one of the most respected media empires in the world—through its most challenging era yet

THE SOLUTION
Stay focused on high-quality journalism as the main source of distinctiveness, but experiment with alternative formats as a way to broaden appeal.

SUSTAINING THE WIN
Pay attention to your critics, who may understand your weaknesses better than you'd like to think.

THOMAS J. USHER: BRINGING U.S. STEEL UP FROM THE SCRAP HEAP

Courtesy of Todd Buchanan

LESSON PLAN

Win in a highly competitive, commoditized industry without moving everything offshore.

Engineer the comeback of a company—and an industry—that has historically resisted cultural and organizational change.

Consolidate to gain the heft to compete globally.

POWER PLAYERS

Thomas J. Usher, chairman and CEO of U.S. Steel, and Wilbur L. Ross Jr., head of the American subsidiary of Arcelor Mittal, the world's largest steelmaker, led a turnaround of their beleaguered behemoths. In doing so, the two also revived the U.S. steel industry, proving an age-old truism: Size matters.

This story by Michael Arndt from 2003 and with a post-2003 update is an authoritative account of US Steel's global turnaround.

FACING AN OBSOLETE BUSINESS MODEL

Few companies ever had such a glorious reign as United States Steel Corp. Created in 1901, it debuted as the world's biggest steelmaker and the first American company to top $1 billion in market capitalization. Over the next 100 years, it produced the steel for the Panama Canal, the Empire State Building, the San Francisco–Oakland Bay Bridge, 911 ships during World War II, the Superdome in New Orleans, railroads, oil pipelines, tin cans, and upwards of 150 million automobiles. The company built cities, altered the national economy, and lifted generations into the middle class.

But as the American steel company entered its second century, it was struggling just to make it through another year. Cheap imports and domestic minimills, with their nonunion payrolls and ultra-efficient shops, were grabbing sales. Customers were disappearing, either transferring work to lower-wage sites outside the United States or simply shutting down. Pension obligations were ballooning, while management clung to a top-heavy bureaucracy and its sprawling mills gobbled up cash for repairs. Import duties helped, but Pittsburgh-based U.S. Steel still lost $218 million in its centennial year, its fourth annual loss in a decade. Its global rank: a humbling tenth place.

A WORLD AWASH IN STEEL

U.S. Steel's comedown is by no means exceptional. With the world awash in steel, three dozen steel companies in the United States have plunged into bankruptcy since 1998, including three of the nation's top five producers and two brand-new minimills. The most recent victim: Weirton Steel Corp., which declared Chapter 11 in May 2003. Over the same period, more than 35,000 steelworkers—one in every three, by the industry's count— have lost their jobs, and the government has been forced to pick up the pensions of some 230,000 retirees and dependents. And even though U.S. steel capacity has shrunk to pre-1993 levels, worldwide capacity now tops 1 billion tons a year, exceeding global demand by an estimated 200 million tons—or twice the annual output of the entire U.S. steel industry. That means that despite the broadest round of steel tariffs in almost 20 years, the carnage is bound to continue.

CONSOLIDATION IS KEY

Lost in this extraordinary tumult, however, is something even more extraordinary: a new American steel industry is rising from the wreckage. In a whirl of deals, an emergent Big Three—minimill king Nucor Corp., upstart International Steel Group Inc., and a resurgent U.S. Steel—have acquired the assets of a half-dozen bankrupt peers, consolidating one of the most stubbornly fragmented industries in basic manufacturing. The trio now accounts for nearly half the steel made in the United States and two-thirds of the sheet steel and other flat-rolled metal that go into vehicles and big-ticket appliances. The three are also going abroad, bidding for mills in Europe and Asia and investing in ventures in South America and Australia. And each wants more. Declares U.S. Steel Chairman and Chief Executive Thomas J. Usher: "This is only the beginning."

Moreover, thanks to a trailblazing deal with organized labor, U.S. Steel and ISG could soon transform themselves into low-cost manufacturers, enabling each of them, like Nucor, to reliably make money in the rough world of international steel. "There is absolutely no doubt that U.S. Steel and ISG will be significantly more competitive with Nucor and globally," says Nucor CEO Daniel R. DiMicco. In fact, ISG is well on its way. The Cleveland-based company, which began only in early 2002 with the idled assets of bankrupt LTV Corp., exported 300,000 tons of hot-rolled steel to China in April—at a profit. Thanks to personnel cuts, ISG is producing a ton of steel per employee every hour, down from 2.4 hours per ton at LTV. "It's a sea change for the industry," says ISG Chairman Wilbur L. Ross Jr.

POWER MOVE

Why consolidate in an industry as capital-intensive as steel? The facilities can't share equipment or materials, and the costs and complexity of distribution will only increase. However, the newly merged outposts will be able to share critical functional expertise in sales, marketing, R&D, and—vital in an industry with such a strong labor presence—human resources.

To be sure, the ascent of the Big Three is likely to be traumatic for both employees and competitors—and a challenge for customers and management alike. Still, the industry restructuring may turn out to be an epochal event, possibly ushering in an age of stability and an end to trade protectionism. Over the next decade, many industry analysts predict, consolidation could leave just six or seven global steel companies standing. By getting into the game today, America's Big Three have a good chance of making it into the lineup.

CHANGE BRINGS CHALLENGES

Many people have already been hurt in the shift. Some 200,000 retirees and dependents have seen their health-care benefits annulled as a result of U.S. Steel's $1.12 billion takeover of bankrupt National Steel Corp. in May and ISG's acquisitions of LTV and Bethlehem Steel Corp. The government's Pension Benefit Guaranty Corp. has picked up these obligations, the largest such transfer in the agency's 29-year history.

Now, to bring labor expenses down further to Nucor's rock-bottom level, the two are planning to eliminate 9,000 more jobs by year-end. Moreover, by boosting productivity and capacity, the three will only intensify the industry shakeout, turning up the heat on other steel producers to match them.

From a customer's perspective, pricing may be another downside. Steel users could be pinched as the Big Three exploit their bulked-up size to tinker with output and shore up prices. Navistar International Corp., for instance, can no longer get the discounts it once did, reports Robert C. Lannert, vice chairman and chief financial officer. Instead, the truck maker is looking into piggybacking its 80,000-ton-a-year steel order with long-time business partner Ford Motor Co. or lining up a permanent supplier from outside the United States. Michael J. Wuest, chief procurement officer for Oshkosh Truck Corp. which buys more than 100,000 tons of steel annually, also laments the new order. "You're never going to see the buyer's market you once did," he says.

Inside the Big Three, the management challenges are also daunting. Each one has to mesh operations and whack expenses without letting quality or reliability slip. The troika must also contend with a three-year-long slide in U.S. manufacturing, which is sapping demand. Then there is the matter of surviving in a world marketplace without government help. After lobbying by all three companies, President George W. Bush imposed tariffs on steel imports in March 2002. And given the drubbing the president took for imposing the tariffs, it's unlikely that he will ride to the industry's rescue if it founders again.

TRIAGE TROUBLE

Some of these issues, including the grief of laid-off workers and impoverished retirees, cannot easily be redressed. But other challenges may be less troublesome than they first appear. Take the recently imposed tariffs. To begin with, imports from Canada, Mexico, Brazil, South Korea, and other nations were exempt. In addition, the White House has granted hundreds of exclusions, so that the tariffs now apply to only 20 percent of imports. The tariffs also have been reduced, as they phase down toward zero. "It's been kind of neutered," says Leo J. Larkin, a metals industry analyst with Standard & Poor's.

> **POWER MOVE**
> Companies benefit when their new partners espouse healthy, productive business practices, and for U.S. Steel, VSZ will do just that. However, simply acquiring assets overseas will not solve U.S. Steel's problems back home. Only significant changes in structures and processes will get this aging company back on its feet.

Postacquisition integrations, too, could go more smoothly than many predict. Nucor, of course, is famous for going head to head with even low-wage producers, thanks to a corporate culture that enshrines productivity. Lately, U.S. Steel's management is showing the same knack. Taking what Usher concedes was a big gamble, the company went overseas for the first time and spent $475 million for Slovakian steelmaker VSZ in 2000. Today, the facility is U.S. Steel's most profitable and the largest producer of flat-rolled steel in Central Europe. ISG's Ross, meanwhile, is a storied contrarian investor who has made a fortune by salvaging bankrupt assets. And to better his chances with ISG, he has enlisted a Nucor alum as chief executive. Investors seem to approve: shares of U.S. Steel and Nucor both have climbed 20 percent in 2003. (ISG is privately held.)

Oddly, a shakeout has been prescribed as the cure-all for the American steel industry for decades. Elsewhere, consolidation did take hold. Over the past decade, steel producers in Europe and Japan have merged into just a handful of giants. Most other basic industries in the United States are also now dominated by a few titans. Yet U.S. steelmakers have remained a multitude of bit players slugging it out against each other. As a result, they've often been no match for foreign companies that, with so much excess capacity, have commandeered 20 percent of the U.S. market.

So why the frenzy of dealmaking today? The catalyst, all agree, was the abrupt shutdown in late 2001 of LTV, then the nation's number four steelmaker. Overnight, 7,500 people were out of work and 82,000 retirees and dependents were on their own. The losses jolted the United Steelworkers of America. Before that, the union had resisted every attempt to reduce pensions or retiree health-care benefits. And for good reason: after decades of cutbacks, the retired outnumbered active employees at old-line companies by an average of 8 to 1. But after LTV's failure, the union leadership concluded that it had better do everything it could to keep other steelmakers from liquidating too, or it would have no dues-paying members at all.

POWER MOVE

Fortunately for U.S. Steel, ISG Chairman Wilbur L. Ross Jr. is a savvy negotiator. Successful bargaining requires more than just a poker face and patience; you need to understand how to create a win—not only for yourself, but also for your opponent.

STRUCTURE AND PROCESS

It takes two to make a deal, however, and no one wanted to bargain with the steelworkers—until Ross came along. He told the union that he would restart LTV, but on two conditions: the steelworkers would have to let him off the hook for the $5 billion in retiree obligations that had helped to sink LTV, and they would have to consent to a new contract allowing him to operate the facilities with far fewer employees. In exchange for profit sharing, a defined-contribution retirement plan, and no pay cuts for rehired workers, the union agreed. Ross closed on his $262 million acquisition in April 2002, through his private-equity investment firm, W.L. Ross & Co. And with Nucor veteran Rodney B. Mott as CEO, ISG began restarting the former LTV mills last summer.

Using its new labor contract as a template, privately held ISG next picked up the assets of Acme Metals Inc. for $65 million in late 2002. Then, in Spring 2003, ISG followed up with its biggest takeover yet, paying $1.5 billion for the assets of Bethlehem Steel, the nation's third-largest steelmaker. With that, ISG leapfrogged U.S. Steel in domestic capacity to rank second behind Nucor. "He accomplished what those of us in the industry couldn't, given all the baggage we carry," notes Robert J. Darnall, former chairman and CEO of Inland Steel Industries Inc. and now a director at U.S. Steel.

Adopting a growth-by-acquisition strategy, Nucor also has been trawling bankruptcy courts for steel assets. Through its steady rise to the top of the American steel industry, the Charlotte-based manufacturer had built all of its facilities. But in late 2002, it snatched up two insolvent minimill rivals—Trico Steel Co. for $117 million and Birmingham Steel Corp. for $615 million—and in March it paid $35 million for a minimill in Arizona that North Star Steel Co. had shuttered. With its new assets, Nucor is expected to reach $6 billion in sales in 2003, up from $4.8 billion last year, with steel shipments topping 16 million tons and profits hitting $105 million.

As its rivals began passing it by, U.S. Steel got busy, too. In addition to purchasing National Steel's assets, U.S. Steel agreed in March to pay $23 million for a second European steelmaker, in Serbia, and is now one of two finalists for Polskie Huty Stali, Poland's giant steelwork, which is being privatized. If U.S. Steel wins the auction, it will be number three in capacity, up from sixth today and eleventh a year ago, with 2003 sales climbing to $10 billion, from $7 billion last year.

CREATE A WIN FOR YOURSELF AND YOUR OPPONENT

Of the new Big Three, U.S. Steel will have to do the heaviest lifting. The company has a salaried workforce of 4,000, plus 1,700 brought over from National Steel, and a seven-tier organizational structure. While its white-collar payroll is down from 27,000 in 1983, Nucor gets by with no more than 1,700 nonproduction employees and has just two layers between CEO DiMicco and any shop-floor worker. ISG is down to four levels, too. Moreover, U.S. Steel will have to root out what even Usher characterizes as "an overseer's mentality," inbred for a century. "U.S. Steel has the potential to regain a lot of strength," states Daniel A. Roling, a metals analyst at Merrill Lynch & Co. "But are they stronger? Not today."

POWER MOVE

Because steel is a commodity, manufacturers can do relatively little to customize products. Instead, to distinguish themselves, companies have to excel in other ways, such as competitive pricing or extraordinary customer service. By eliminating organizational levels, Usher will not only reduce costs, but move toward a much-needed entrepreneurial, egalitarian culture.

Indeed, Roling estimates that U.S. Steel will lose $26 million in 2003.

Usher & Co., however, say that they will prevail—and sooner than outsiders might think. By year-end, the company plans to weed out one of every five administrative employees. Seniority won't necessarily be the deciding factor in who will go. "The people who are left will be people who can adapt to the new model," Usher vows. Those who prefer yesterday's command-and-control mind-set, he adds, "will enjoy their retirement." The inner circle also shows no doubts about the company's wherewithal to pay its bills. A junk-grade debtor, the company already owes $175 million a year in interest, at rates of up to 10.75 percent, and its long-term debt of $1.9 billion is bigger than its market cap. But U.S. Steel has no big debt payments due before 2008. And if it needs more cash, it has $600 million in revolving credit as well as coal mines and other noncore assets that it can unload.

All told, U.S. Steel figures that by year-end it will be able to chop $550 million from its preacquisition expenses of $9.65 billion. That would lower its breakeven point by $30 a ton and, based on analysis by Morgan Stanley & Co. , lift its 2004 earnings by $310 million. Roling, too, sees better earnings in 2004. He bumped his price target for U.S. Steel to $20 a share, from $15.50 today.

The race isn't over, of course. ISG's Ross, in partnership with Goldman Sachs & Co., is bidding $250 million for bankrupt Kia Steel Co. of South Korea. Nucor, meantime, is investing in joint ventures in Brazil and Australia. And U.S. Steel executives are checking out other domestic steelmakers that already are bankrupt or close to it, including Ford's former in-house supplier, Rouge Industries Inc. All of which lends credence to the idea that within several years, the international steel industry could be down to a half-dozen giants. At the moment, hardly anyone is ruling the Americans out.

TURNAROUND REALIZED

In 2003, as U.S. Steel CEO Usher was boosting the company's heft through acquisitions, John P. Surma was right there with him, as chief financial officer. In 2004, Surma succeeded Usher as chief executive, and today he is also U.S. Steel's chairman.

U.S. Steel now ranks third in domestic steel output and seventh worldwide. It has doubled its revenues since 2002 to $14.04 billion in 2005. The company has been solidly profitable for the last two years and is expected to net more than $1 billion in 2006. It has 46,000 employees and owes retirement benefits to 114,000 former workers and beneficiaries.

But Surma, 51, an accountant who logged 23 years at Price Waterhouse, isn't the dealmaker Usher was. The company lost in its bidding for Poland's steel combine, to Mittal Steel. It passed, meantime, on making a formal pitch for Rouge Industries, which ended up getting sold to a Russian company. Since then, U.S. Steel executives have said they've sized up some of China's steelmakers but have not made any offers.

Back in Usher's time, the company said in its 10K filings with the government that management's strategy was to expand globally. In its most recent 10K, that language is gone. Instead, U.S. Steel lays out its strategy like this: "to be a conservative, responsible company."

While Surma has backed off on acquisitions, however, his peers have kept at it. Since 2004, Nucor's DiMicco has bought the assets of four minimills around the United States for a total of $325 million. In addition, Nucor has begun producing iron—a substitute for scrap metal which the company has historically used to make steel— through joint ventures in Brazil and Australia.

Nucor is still lean. Though its revenues have tripled since 2001 to $12.7 billion in 2005, it employs just 11,300 people, with only 66 at its corporate headquarters in Charlotte. That's one big reason why the company has surpassed U.S. Steel to become the nation's most-profitable steelmaker, with net income of $1.31 billion in 2005 and $1.69 billion in 2006, according to analysts' forecasts.

Ross has outdone even DiMicco. In early 2004, he took International Steel Group public and then, 10 months later, agreed to sell the entire outfit to Mittal Steel, a Netherlands-incorporated giant founded and run by Lakshmi N. Mittal. The deal, valued at $4.1 billion excluding debt, created not only America's biggest steelmaker; it vaulted Mittal to the top of the global industry, with 2005 revenue of $28.1 billion and steel shipments of 49.2 million tons.

Mittal Steel, originally known as Ispat International, moved into the U.S. market in 1998 with its takeover of Inland Steel Co.

And Mittal hardly paused after its acquisition of ISG: In mid-2006, after a protracted battle, it bought its European archrival and the world's number. 2 steelmaker, Arcelor of Luxembourg, for roughly $32 billion. The combined company, Arcelor Mittal, is the first to top 100 million tons in annual steel production and was projected to top $85 billion in sales in 2006. Ross is on the board of directors and one of Arcelor Mittal's largest shareholders.

THE PROBLEM
Reviving ailing companies in one of the nation's oldest, most cost-competitive commoditized industries

THE SOLUTION
Consolidate with other steel companies that can help you achieve the economies of scale you need if you are to survive.

Remove layers to increase efficiency and decrease bureaucracy.

SUSTAINING THE WIN
Continue to acquire assets abroad.

Work closely to learn from these companies' successes and help them avoid your failures.

ALAN MULALLY:
A PLAN TO MAKE FORD FLY

Courtesy of Getty Images.

Turn around one of the world's most famous—and famously troubled—corporations.

Apply lessons from an industry with similar engineering and operational issues, but vastly different sales and marketing challenges.

Find a way to finance a turnaround—when your credit rating has already taken a nosedive.

Move quickly to develop a vision for success and action plans to achieve it.

POWER PLAYER

Having saved the day at Boeing, Alan Mulally now faces an even tougher challenge at Ford, as the formerly great American automaker is in need of a complete overhaul. Ford's shareholders, managers, and employees hope that Mulally is just the one to lead it.

In one of the top stories from September 2006, David Welch, David Kiley, and Stanley Holmes take a close look at "Ford's Latest Recall."

REINVENTING A GIANT

Some kids, from the very start, believe they are destined for greatness. Alan R. Mulally was one of them. As a lad in Lawrence, Kansas, he sat in the front pew at church, the better to study how the minister revved up the congregation. When he was 17, Mulally considered President John F. Kennedy's call to send Americans to the moon a personal message for him. "I got in front of the TV and said, 'I'm ready,'" Mulally once recalled in an interview with *BusinessWeek*. He signed up for extra classes in science, math, and chemistry. He even took flying lessons.

Mulally never made it into orbit. But he found plenty of space to nurture his ambitions at Boeing Co., where he arrived as a junior engineer in a VW Beetle in 1969 and eventually ascended to president and CEO of its fabled commercial airplane division. Now he is taking on a challenge that may be even more daunting than putting a man on the moon: turning around the ailing Ford Motor Co. as its new CEO.

The youthful-looking, enthusiastic, sometimes temperamental 61-year-old executive has not been on anybody's list of hot CEO candidates since the late 1990s, when he was offered top jobs at Raytheon Co. and Teledesic, a failed commercial satellite company. Nor was Mulally Ford's first choice. Since taking the CEO job himself in late 2001, Chairman William C. Ford Jr. has tried several times to find someone to take it off his hands, going after such industry luminaries as Renault-Nissan CEO Carlos Ghosn and DaimlerChrysler Chairman Dieter Zetsche. The fact that he has had to go outside of the auto world to fill the post raises a profound question: can a non-car guy fix Ford?

Mulally brings with him knowledge that will be invaluable as he straps on his seat belt at Ford. Boeing is an old-line industrial giant that has endured epic problems and successfully reinvented itself. Mulally has made brilliant product strategy decisions, in particular his big bet on the fuel-sipping 787 rather than the gas-guzzlers favored by archrival Airbus. He has experience dealing with unions, though not all of it is positive. He is also something of a turnaround artist. After September 11, he quickly slashed more than 30,000 jobs, closed plants, and kept his unit in the black. And somehow Mulally has managed to spend the last three-and-a-half decades at one of

America's most scandal-prone companies without getting much mud on his reputation. "I've been in some tough situations," Mulally told *BusinessWeek*. "I'm here to help a great company continue to survive."

But the former engineer also has significant gaps in his résumé. It's clear that he has never faced anything like the challenges he'll see at Ford. For starters, this is a much larger company than the division he ran at Boeing—with six times as many employees, eight brands vs. one, and 110 plants worldwide vs. 6. Boeing launches a new line of airplanes about every 13 years. Ford cranks out new car models every few months. Boeing does almost no consumer marketing, while Ford is one of the biggest advertisers in the land. Finance isn't a particularly strong suit for Mulally, which is a little worrying at a company bobbing in a sea of red ink. And, finally, he has never had the high public profile typical of auto executives. If anything, Ford's new CEO is averse to the limelight and tends to be thin-skinned.

BREAKING THE CURSE OF THE INTERLOPER

At Ford, Mulally is going to have to get used to a very hot glare. The company's sales are in free fall, and it has lost $1.4 billion so far this year—with further losses sure to come. His supporting cast is made up mostly of the same executives who have failed to pull the company out of its current tailspin. These people may resent his outsider status and actively try to thwart him. Yet Mulally will have to depend on them while learning the car business on the fly. He'll also have the omnipresent Ford family looking over his shoulder, not to mention the United Auto Workers.

Perhaps even tougher, Mulally will have to break the interloper's curse. Few outsiders get top jobs in the auto business, and Detroit has a nasty way of chewing them up. In the 1990s, brand managers like Bausch & Lomb executive Ronald L. Zarella and a host of other consumer-goods marketers tried to fix General Motors Corp. Ford hired plenty of people with similar résumés, only to see them fail. By 2002, most of them were gone.

Mulally "is not that anchored in the industry. He doesn't even know what he doesn't know," says Jeffrey A. Sonnenfeld, senior associate dean at the Yale School of Management. But his status as an outsider also has some upside. "You're not married to the prevailing models of an industry," Sonnenfeld adds.

By hiring Mulally, however, Ford is getting a manufacturing maestro with few industrial peers. If there's one thing Mulally is good at, it's taking a broken or underperforming production system, figuring out what's wrong with it, and then making it better than it ever was.

Nothing tested his skills like the production meltdown that nearly sent Boeing crashing to earth in 1997. At the time, the company was trying to boost efficiency on the entire production line, even as it was ramping up to take advantage of a flood of orders. The system collapsed under the strain, costing the company $2.6 billion and forcing it to post its first annual loss in half a century.

USE A SIMPLE PLAN TO TACKLE COMPLEX PROBLEMS

Enter Mulally, who had just been named chief of the commercial aircraft division. He quickly identified the causes: inefficient production techniques, poor supplier relationships, overly ambitious airplane delivery targets, and a culture that encouraged managers to hide problems. Mulally attacked these interrelated problems with a simple plan that had clear productivity targets. Within weeks of his arrival, he gave airplane production managers responsibility for profit and loss, a first at Boeing. "We celebrated every delivery and every production increase," Mulally told *BusinessWeek* in an interview in 2001. By 1999, orders had nearly doubled to 620 planes, and operating margins were up fivefold.

Ford badly needs a manufacturing Mr. Fix-It. The company has the lowest utilization of its plants of any automaker, according to Harbour Consulting. Ford used only 79 percent of its capacity last year, compared with 90 percent for GM and 94 percent for Chrysler Group, while Toyota ran at 106 percent. Ford also has the dubious distinction of being the least productive automaker in terms of man-hours per vehicle, an hour worse than GM and five hours worse than Nissan Motor Co. "Ford has not invested in, nor focused on, productivity gains in recent years to the same level as its competitors, and it has cost the company real money," says Ron Harbour. Here's one place where Mulally has an opportunity to make shareholders smile.

Mulally's turnaround experience will be critical at Ford. The rebound that he engineered at Boeing's commercial division came to an abrupt halt on September 11, 2001. After orders for new airplanes nose-dived, he swung into action, closing several plants and renegotiating delivery schedules for some 500 airplanes. As business recovered, he kept his unit in the black.

This turnaround experience is going to be critical at Ford, which has botched the restructuring that began under Bill Ford five years ago. The company has not acted swiftly enough to cut its head count and get its productivity up. Meanwhile, the restructuring blueprint keeps changing. Ford said in January that it would cut at least 25,000 jobs and close 14 plants in North America by 2012. Then last month Ford said that it would cut fourth-quarter production by 21 percent because of falling demand. An announcement speeding up that schedule of closures is expected this month.

> **POWER MOVE**
>
> Mulally's expertise at managing through tough times will definitely come into use. Although eliminating tens of thousands of employees is never an enviable task, it is one that the ailing automaker can no longer avoid. Mulally needs to inspire confidence in the market—a task that will hardly be possible if he doesn't take immediate steps to regain profitability.

INSPIRE CONFIDENCE IN A CHANGING MARKET

Mulally's ability to cut Ford down to the right size is going to depend upon securing cooperation from the UAW. It's a union with a much louder bark and toothier bite than the International Association of Machinists he worked with at Boeing. Yes, the UAW is a somewhat diminished force. But the union can still make matters ugly for Ford.

Perhaps Mulally has learned something from the strike that shut down many of Boeing's plants for 23 days last year. After all, his hard-nosed bargaining was largely responsible for the stoppage. In the days before the Machinists walked off the job, Mulally thought he had shrewdly divided the union along generational lines. By offering hefty bonuses and retirement goodies, he hoped to entice younger workers to sign on. A similar strategy had worked in 2002. But not this time. Mulally was forced to negotiate a settlement that gave the union most of what it wanted.

With that memory still fresh in labor circles, Mulally will have to tread warily with the UAW. Ford needs to downsize as fast as it can. Traditionally, the UAW has been cool to drastic job cuts. But the direness of Ford's situation is apparent to even militant unionistas.

Says David Cole, who runs the Center for Automotive Research: "I'd be surprised if they can't get something very constructive hammered out."

While Mulally has plenty of relevant background in manufacturing and labor relations, he has precious little in finance. At a time of financial crisis, Mulally will have to lean on Ford's financial whizzes, including Kenneth Leet, the former Goldman Sachs banker brought in to consult on asset sales and other strategic financial matters. Not only does Ford need to restore the balance sheet by making tough decisions, but the company also requires someone who can calm Wall Street and the rating agencies, which have pushed Ford into junk territory. That role doesn't come naturally to Mulally.

POWER MOVE

Fortunately for Mulally, Ford has a long history of hiring some of the country's most accomplished financiers. Robert McNamara, for example, later became President John F. Kennedy's secretary of defense. However, Mulally must still take the lead in balancing the company's financial and strategic objectives. The cash may seem critical now, but maintaining a controlling position in Ford Motor Credit Co. may be critical to long-term success.

BALANCE FINANCIAL AND STRATEGIC OBJECTIVES

Mulally's relations with Wall Street have never been particularly strong. While he has laid off thousands of people, sold off small manufacturing units, and whittled down Boeing's production capacity, Mulally has never negotiated or managed a major merger or acquisition. And when Boeing sold a Wichita plant in 2005, the pressure to do so came from former Boeing CEO Harry Stonecipher, not Mulally.

This is not a moment to shy away from tough financial decisions at Ford. The company lost $1.4 billion in the first half of the year. And the second half looks to be even worse. With analysts worried about falling sales, expect the bottom line to get pummeled in the second half. Morgan Stanley analyst Himanshu Patel says the cuts will boost losses to Ford's North American business to $4 billion for the year. The company's North American business alone has already lost $1.3 billion in the first half of the year.

All eyes are on Ford's cash burn. The company spent $1.5 billion of its hoard in the first six months of the year. While rating agencies stress that Ford has about $23.6 billion in cash to cover new-car development, restructuring charges, and retiree costs, the cash drain will only accelerate once the automaker unveils yet another restructuring this month. Ford has already spent $700 million on separation packages and paid layoff expenses for union workers. Fitch & Co. analyst Mark Oline says that between the added restructuring costs and the operating losses, Ford will burn $7 billion in cash this year. Ford's B+ junk credit rating is already on credit watch with negative implications—and Standard & Poor's will decide this month if another downgrade is needed.

Yes, Mulally has enough cash to keep Ford afloat for some time—but not indefinitely. That's one reason why management is shopping its luxury brands. Even the idea of selling 51 percent of its profitable Ford Motor Credit Co. finance business has been floated.

Why does Ford need the cash? Even if the next round of restructuring stems the losses, its revenues are expected to keep falling. They're down $7 billion, to $83 billion, in the first half of the year. If that isn't stabilized, Oline says, Ford will have a tough time slowing the cash burn. And even though its pension fund in the United States is underfunded by only $2 billion, the company still lives with the risk that a downturn in the equity markets could force it to pony up more cash. Since 2004, Ford has paid $5.3 billion in cash into its pension funds.

INSPIRED DIRECTION

Mulally has earned high marks in the aerospace industry for his stewardship of two of Boeing's most successful projects, the 777 jet and, more recently, the game-changing lightweight 787. But developing smart products at an auto company, especially one with huge holes in its model lineup, is an entirely different proposition. In an interview with *BusinessWeek*, an upbeat Bill Ford insisted that Mulally would get plenty of support. "Alan will have all the help he needs from inspired car guys," said Ford. "What our inspired car guys need is inspired direction."

POWER MOVE

Mulally's fearlessness was well suited to pushing through projects at Boeing, but its suitability to Ford's culture remains to be seen. Like every new leader, he will have to move with confidence in his early days, but as an industry outsider, he will have to take care to avoid violating any long-standing industry norms.

Mulally demonstrated gold-plated leadership managing the 777 and 787 projects. The 777 was a gutsy attack on conventional wisdom. Plenty of safety experts believed that twin-engine planes couldn't safely fly over the vastness of the Pacific Ocean. But Mulally pushed ahead—developing a plan, getting his troops to buy in, then focusing relentlessly on executing his vision. He has brought the same zeal to the 787 project.

These are impressive feats, but they're quite unlike the product and marketing challenges that Mulally has inherited at Ford. Boeing's commercial aircraft division is essentially a B2B manufacturer; it builds planes for airlines and cargo haulers. For the most part, Ford is a consumer brand, and a badly degraded one at that. To excite buyers, it needs somebody who understands car color and fashion trends, things that don't matter much to aircraft manufacturers.

POWER MOVE

Mulally needs a winning strategy for Ford—fast. Even if he can't replace as many models as its peers this year, he can certainly begin remaking Ford's identity—a task that may be operationally easier, but creatively far more difficult. Although the company has spent decades successfully being all things to all people, in an increasingly connected, competitive world, Ford can no longer be the jack-of-all-trades. Instead, it needs to find its new niche among the dozens of players in the market today.

Ford's dire financial situation notwithstanding, what has investors and analysts most concerned is the automaker's continued inability to come up with hit products. Sales of the company's bread-and-butter SUVs and trucks are sliding amid high gasoline prices, but Ford can't seem to build passenger cars that people want. Merrill Lynch & Co. analyst John Murphy says that in the next three years, only 60 percent of Ford's models will be replaced. That compares poorly with 80 percent at GM and 83 percent at Toyota. The upshot, according to Murphy: Ford will lose about one percentage point of market share a year until 2010. There's not much Mulally can do about that, since it takes about five years for Ford to get a vehicle from drawing board to showroom.

ENSURE THAT THE PRODUCT MATCHES THE MARKETING

"Going to market" is a phrase that auto executives understand all too well, but it may take a while to fully resonate with the Boeing transplant. And Ford is a marketing nightmare. Not only has the message bounced all over the place, but the company must overcome a prevailing sentiment among consumers that the quality of its products just can't stack up against the Japanese. The fact that Ford's quality has improved in recent years simply hasn't registered with the driving public. The stick-to-it Mulally may be able to impose some consistency on the marketing message, but restoring luster to a fabled brand will take a marketing genius.

MONDAY MORNING...

THE PROBLEM
Leading the turnaround of one of the world's most publicly scrutinized companies—as an industry outsider

THE SOLUTION
Take immediate action to return the company to profitability.

Negotiate carefully with union leaders to avoid irreparably costly standoffs.

Apply lessons in operational efficiency learned at prior positions.

SUSTAINING THE WIN
Work quickly to establish both a short-term triage plan and a long-term vision for success.

BRIAN FRANCE:
THE PRINCE OF NASCAR

Broaden the company's appeal without alienating its traditional fan base.

Invest heavily to challenge antitrust lawsuits, but maintain focus on new growth opportunities.

POWER PLAYER

Patriarch Bill France, his son Brian, and his daughter Lesa run the lucrative franchise amid rising complaints that they are monopolizing the sport. Brian France, chairman and CEO of NASCAR, must modernize the company's traditional tactics to sustain the company's growth.

This piece is a revealing 2004 portrait by Tom Lowry of the powerful France family that rules U.S. stock-car racing.

133

TRADITION

The smell of gasoline, the roar of engines, gruff men puffing on cigarettes and cussing about needing more horsepower out on the oval. For most people, that's hardly the stuff of childhood memories. But Brian France isn't most people. When the son of America's first family of stock-car racing thinks back as far as he can, he is a four-year-old with a mop of sandy hair tagging along as his daddy chews the fat with daredevil drivers such as Richard Petty and grease-stained pit crews in the garages of Daytona International Speedway. Or he is looking up at politicians and movie stars who have stopped by the France house in the days just before the Daytona 500. They sip cocktails and pat him on the head.

In his 41 years, France can't recall not being at Daytona, the Sunday spectacle that marks the start of yet another NASCAR season. But this year's big race, on February 15, will be like no other for the husky, baby-faced France—and not just because President George W. Bush is scheduled to make an appearance. Race Day 2004 will be Brian's first as the chairman and chief executive officer of a zooming, multibillion-dollar empire founded on the sands of Daytona Beach, Florida, in 1948 by his grandfather, William "Big Bill" France Sr.

OVER-THE-TOP IN EVERYTHING

Last September, Brian's father, 70-year-old Bill Jr., announced that after 20 years of being prepped in various executive posts, his son was being raised to the NASCAR throne. That came as a surprise to the racing world because Bill Jr., now a billionaire, had ruled the sport with an iron fist since succeeding his own father in 1972. Heart surgery and bouts with cancer in recent years may have influenced the decision. "Bill decided," one confidant explains, "that he wanted to be around for the transition."

What Brian inherits is a humming media and marketing machine that keeps swiftly evolving from its start as a pastime for beer-guzzling Bubbas. TV deals worth $2.8 billion with Fox, NBC, and TNT extend out to 2008, and NASCAR races are drawing the second-largest sports-viewing audience after the NFL. Thirteen million fans bought tickets to the 2,200 races in NASCAR's various divisions last year, with an average turnout of 186,000 for big events—at an average ticket price of $75.

The numbers don't stop there. In the past five years, four new tracks have opened in big urban areas, including Los Angeles and Chicago, and plans are coming together to put one in New York City—or at least nearby. Corporations spend more than $1 billion a year for NASCAR sponsorships and promotions, and annual sales of NASCAR-licensed merchandise top $2 billion.

NASCAR executives are relentless self-promoters who like to say that the sport has 75 million fans, more than half of them hard-core. Even if that assessment is over the top, NASCAR certainly has become a cultural force as politicians scurry to curry favor with a powerful demographic of white males dubbed "NASCAR dads." No wonder Bush, a no-show at the World Series and the Super Bowl, is headed for Daytona.

There is a faint grinding sound, however, beneath the sweet purr of the NASCAR engine. Even before the steering wheel was out of Bill Jr.'s hands, racing's old guard was privately questioning whether Brian has the right stuff to run the sport. After all, Bill Jr. is revered for putting NASCAR on the national map while fiercely guarding the interests of drivers, team owners, and track proprietors (along with those of the Frances, of course), and doing so with a cozy family feel. Racing insiders like to say that Big Bill turned stock cars into a sport, Bill Jr. turned them into a business, and now Brian wants to turn them into entertainment. It's the lure of Hollywood that has folks nervous. But the younger France, who shares a home in Los Angeles with his second wife and his 11-year-old stepdaughter, vows to shake things up so the sport doesn't stagnate.

STEPPING OUT OF THE COMFORT ZONE

France doesn't kid himself about how much he will be scrutinized. "Am I here because of my last name? To a degree," says France. " But I would ask people to judge me and my executive team on what we accomplish. You never want to alienate the core fans, but we are going to take risks."

It's not just a debate over the glitzing of NASCAR that could be troublesome. The Frances face an antitrust suit alleging that they unfairly use their control over NASCAR, stock-car racing's sanctioning and rule-making body, to favor the family-controlled but publicly held racetrack company International Speedway Corp.

in the awarding of events. The lawsuit, filed by a shareholder of another racetrack company, is set to go to trial this summer in Texas. It could shine the glare of publicity on France family secrets—especially since David Boies, the lawyer who prosecuted the Justice Department's case against Microsoft Corp., represents the Frances, while O. J. Simpson defense attorney Johnnie Cochran represented the shareholder.

Tragically, Johnnie Cochran died of a brain tumor in early 2005. His law firm continues to represent the shareholder who is suing the Frances. In early 2006, a federal judge turned down a request by NASCAR and ISC to dismiss the lawsuit, instead ruling that the antitrust complaint met the test of sufficiency. The two sides can use the next year to gather information, and the case will be heard later in the year.

Meanwhile, in a sport that never met a sponsor it didn't like, France will have to persuade corporations to keep spending. With the sponsorship costs of maintaining a competitive racing team going through the roof—they have more than doubled in 10 years, to as much as $15 million per season—and with marketing messages being lost among the increasing clutter of logos on race suits, cars, and tracks, that will be a distinct challenge. Several teams have struggled to find sponsors this year. "The costs and clutter are going up," says independent analyst Dennis McAlpine, who follows ISC. Still, Brian intends to aggressively pursue two industries that have been elusive: financial services and high tech.

BROADEN THE APPEAL

In tech, anyway, he made one giant step even before his ascension. In June 2003, it was announced that after 32 years, Winston was being succeeded as the sponsor of NASCAR's premier racing series by Nextel Communications Inc. Winston parent R.J. Reynolds Tobacco Holdings Inc. had been

POWER MOVE

France wants to broaden NASCAR's appeal—a seemingly paradoxical move for a company that succeeded in the past by proudly advertising its deep southern roots. Targeting industries with the opposite problem—extending their reach beyond their coastal homelands—is a good first step. However, even with the best-laid plans, France may not be able to expand along so many dimensions at once: age, gender, race, class, geography, and even nationality.

paying roughly $30 million a year, but the Reston (Virginia) wireless outfit is shelling out $750 million over 10 years to put its name on the Nextel Cup Series—one of the biggest sponsorship deals ever. That a technology company is replacing a struggling cigarette maker speaks volumes about where the sport is headed. Working with Nextel, NASCAR can now exploit opportunities to sell racing to teenagers, something it couldn't do with Winston.

That's in keeping with France's push to lure younger fans. NASCAR is in the first year of a six-year exclusive video-game deal with Electronic Arts (some drivers, like Dale Earnhardt Jr., use the games' racing simulator to bone up on their skills). EA is talking with Nextel about offering some kind of NASCAR game on its phones. Nextel already offers a special news feed, NASCAR on the go, to its phone subscribers. And nascar.com is one of the five most heavily trafficked sports Web sites.

Like any big family, the Frances are not without internal tensions. Brian has heard whispers for years that his older sister and only sibling, Lesa France Kennedy, 42, the president of ISC, is the sharper executive. It doesn't help that Lesa graduated from Duke and Brian never got his degree from Central Florida. Despite the sibling rivalry, NASCAR insiders say that both Brian and Lesa knew that appointing a woman to run male-dominated NASCAR was not going to happen. And France is wasting no time in making it clear that the Era of Brian has begun.

France's first directive was announcing on January 20 rule changes in NASCAR's point system, which determines the champion driver every year. The changes were meant to create more excitement in October and November, the tail end of the 10-month season, when TV ratings get hammered by pro football. After all, NASCAR's version of the Super Bowl, the Daytona 500, starts the season instead of ending it.

BROADEN THE PLAYING FIELD

Messing with a point system that had been in place since 1975 was heresy to some drivers. NASCAR 2003 champ Matt Kenseth and four-time champ Jeff Gordon criticized the changes as being all about ratings, not racing. "You could say that his changes . . . are too far to the entertainment side," says Gordon. Brian's response: NASCAR is entertainment.

The way France sees it, NASCAR isn't just competing with other auto-racing events, such as the open-wheel Indy car series, or with "stick and ball" leagues, but with all entertainment choices.

POWER MOVE

In addition to extending its physical reach, NASCAR has to reposition its content for new audiences. For example, highlighting the physically rigorous nature of the races makes NASCAR appeal more to traditional sports spectators, who enjoy watching sports programs that highlight athletic skill.

That's why he has hired Richard Glover, a former number two executive at ESPN Inc., to forge new relationships with Hollywood. A NASCAR Imax movie will debut in March, and cable channel FX is planning a reality series following the lives of drivers. And NASCAR boasts celebrities galore. California Governor Arnold Schwarzenegger is a fan. So is Ben Affleck, grand marshal of this year's Daytona 500. Sheryl Crow likes the races. Britney, too. "If we can showcase the drama and athleticism differently and in a better way, then that is what it is all about," says Brian.

REPOSITION THE CONTENT

Tinseltown is a long way from stock-car racing's roots in the dirt tracks of the South, where bootleggers, good ol' boys, and veterans just back from World War II swigged a clear liquid that wasn't water and tried to run each other off the road. "Big Bill" France, a Daytona gas station owner, began to put some order into the races, organizing events that ran on the hard sands of the nearby beach. As the races spread throughout the South and onto hard tracks, Big Bill, a formidable figure at 6 feet 5 inches, became troubled that each track had its own rules. So he called a meeting of race organizers at the Streamline Hotel in Daytona in 1947 to suggest that a single entity control stock-car racing. A year later, NASCAR was born.

Through the years, as stock-car racing grew, so did the France family's grip. Today that control is creating an undercurrent of resentment. Plenty of folks in the NASCAR world are hoping that the antitrust suit filed by Plano (Texas) businessman Francis Ferko, a shareholder in Speedway Motorsports Inc., could force the Frances to divest some of their holdings. Ferko contends that before Speedway built the $150 million Texas Motor Speedway in 1997 ($100 million in renovations have been added since), the Frances promised to place two major races there. So far, the track has only one Nextel Cup race.

Ferko alleges that the Frances use NASCAR to unfairly award more races to the tracks owned by ISC, which host 16 of the 36 Nextel races. Two more are run at a track that the family owns separately. While there is supposed to be a Chinese wall between Brian's NASCAR and Lesa's ISC, there is only plasterboard separating them: the operations share the same offices on the same floor in a Daytona building whose facade is done up like a checkered flag. "It's 1,000 percent unfair—or could it be even more unfair?" quips Speedway CEO O. Bruton Smith, the second-largest car dealer in the country, with headquarters in Charlotte. "The greed factor here has been a real problem." Driver Gordon says that concerns that the Frances have too much control are real, but "what they have accomplished allows a lot of us to live some pretty amazing lives."

Both sides say that they want to see the case go to trial. And while Brian and Lesa are putting on a unified front, they've had their share of disagreements over the years. Lesa—who was adopted by Bill Jr. and his wife, Betty Jane—and Brian are anything but effusive about each other. "We do run into heavy competitive situations," says Lesa, who is married to plastic surgeon Bruce Kennedy. For instance, Lesa says that Brian was not thrilled when she negotiated a deal for Pepsi to become the official soft drink of ISC. Coca-Cola Co. is a NASCAR sponsor. "There are always good, spirited debates on how to do things," says Brian.

CRACKING THE BIGGEST MARKET

These days, though, a top priority for both Brian and Lesa is building a track in New York. Stock-car racing in the Big Apple has been talked about for years, but there is a new urgency for NASCAR. On February 6, ISC announced its intention to build a track in Washington State, leaving New York as NASCAR's last major geographic void—and perhaps its most important market. Says NASCAR COO George Pyne, 38, a graduate of Choate and Brown and one of the thirty-odd executives with whom Brian has surrounded himself: "Ten million Americans live in that market. To have a totally successful product, you have to be there."

Building a track in New York will come down to real estate because at a minimum, several hundred acres of land will be needed. Brian spent some 60 days in New York last year promoting the plan, and since ISC would develop the track, Lesa has been flying into town every other week to work on the deal, too. Being in New York would put stock-car racing in Madison Avenue's face, she says: "It would just open a lot of doors."

Nobody would enjoy seeing a track in the city more than the TV network executives who ponied up for NASCAR rights. Until 2001, those rights were negotiated by each racetrack, but France and his top TV executive, Paul Brooks, 38, persuaded track owners to consolidate those rights with NASCAR and strike a network package that included televising all races in the Nextel and second-tier Busch Series. It worked, prompting a shift from cable to the broader broadcast audience. News Corp.'s Fox has made the biggest investment in NASCAR, broadcasting Nextel Cup races in the first half of the season (so as not to conflict with its NFL programming in the fall), putting Busch Series races on its FX channel, covering auto racing extensively on its SPEED Channel, and airing a daily show, *Totally NASCAR*, on its Fox Sports Networks. "We've done a great job of being able to demystify the races with great analysis . . . and all sorts of new camera angles," says Fox Sports CEO David Hill. "And we are able to capture the sounds. These cars sound like caged, prehistoric beasts. It's like nothing else you've heard."

Fox's Winston races (Nextel this year) have averaged a 4 or 5 rating (about 5.4 million households tuning in), vs. about 10.5 for the average Fox NFL game. Still, that's far ahead of baseball's regular-season average 2.6 rating on Fox. Last year's Daytona 500 on Fox posted a 9.8 rating (though, by contrast, this year's Super Bowl on CBS did a 41.4). "Because these are cars we all drive, Dodges, Fords, and Chevrolets," says Hill, "there is an accessibility to it." But not for everybody.

SPONSORS, SPONSORS EVERYWHERE

The rap against auto racing as a TV sport is that it is deathly boring to watch cars go round and round, that people are really only tuned in to see crashes—like folks waiting for the fights during hockey games. Yet fans say that once you understand the race, it's all about strategy. "I see it as a huge, three-dimensional chess game," says Dan Gronich, chairman of real estate firm Grubb & Ellis/New York. "You see how drivers handle drafting [a vacuum created by a front-running car pulling others behind it], passing, pit stops, tire changes. The layers are what make it fascinating." NBC Sports President Ken Schanzer concedes that it may take "some initiation," but "let's face it, NASCAR is putting on a Super Bowl every week."

There is such a thing as too much spectacle, though. And while NASCAR bills itself as the best marketing opportunity in sports, it could be running up against a saturation problem. For the 2004 season, NASCAR will have 36 official sponsors, from the Official Armed Service (the U.S. Army) to the Official Pizza Delivery (Domino's Inc.). Twenty-one other companies, from Ragú to Waste Management Inc., are promotional partners. Each race car has a primary sponsor—which puts up anywhere from $9 million to $15 million per season—and a slew of associate sponsors. The racetracks have separate sponsorships. In addition, drivers can strike their own sponsorship deals. (Star driver Gordon, for one, makes more than $20 million a year in race purses and promotional contracts.)

So is hooking up with stock-car racing really a good investment? That depends on whom you talk to. "Listen, let's say the NASCAR fan base isn't 75 million, but 40 million," says Mark Schweitzer, senior vice president for marketing at Nextel. "There is still tremendous upside for us." David F. D'Alessandro, chairman of John Hancock Financial Services Inc., doesn't see it that way. "To struggle for space with the dozens of other sponsors isn't worth it," he says. "Plus, your main decal is traveling at 200 mph. Who can see that? And is the crowd really sober enough to see it? Having a guy emerge from a fireball isn't a prudent way to sell insurance anyway."

> **POWER MOVE**
>
> Like other entertainment companies, NASCAR has to meet the needs of notoriously skittish advertisers who pull dollars at the first hint of impropriety. The companies and industries best suited for NASCAR sponsorship are those that not only tolerate but thrive on speed, risk, and endurance.

DON'T ALIENATE THE CORE

The overpowering commercialization of NASCAR worries some old-timers, too. "[Brian] always needs to remind himself this is about the race cars," says Richard Petty, 66, a seven-time NASCAR champion and current team owner. But Brian France doesn't need reminding about the footprints he must fill. The family legacy stares back at him every day from the walls of NASCAR's offices: photos of his grandfather and father with drivers, big-shot CEOs, and presidents.

On a recent morning, Brian was in his corner office reviewing the rough cut of a new commercial on a massive flat-screen TV. Using computer-generated images, old drivers are seen next to the new generation—Richard Petty with Gordon, "Fireball" Roberts and David Pearson with Earnhardt Jr.—with the old cars racing against the new machines. The ad's message, that NASCAR is timeless, is Brian's attempt to bridge the old and the new.

"Brian's biggest challenge isn't any of these issues with drivers or sponsors or new fans. His biggest challenge is to be Brian France," says team owner Felix Sabates, who has known him since he was a kid. When the announcer calls out, "Start your engines," at Daytona on February 15, the new CEO will officially get his chance.

MONDAY MORNING...

THE PROBLEM
Fueling organic growth outside of core geographic markets, which are increasingly saturated

THE SOLUTION
Choose your sponsors and target customers carefully to maximize return on investment.

SUSTAINING THE WIN
Maintain your distance from other family-controlled businesses.

Reposition your core value proposition to appeal to different demographics.

EDOUARD MICHELIN: TAKING MICHELIN TO NEW HEIGHTS

Courtesy of Getty Images.

Increase already high margins on a premium product.

Inject new operating routines and policies into a staid, traditional company without damaging its fierce national identity.

POWER PLAYER

Edouard Michelin (recently deceased), heir to his family's legendary tire company, assumed the throne and was shaking things up. After decades of leadership by his father and grandfather, the young CEO had the opportunity to modernize the inveterate French manufacturer.

This profile from 2002, reported from around the globe by Christine Tierney with Ann Therese Palmer, Chester Dawson, and Joann Muller, focuses on scion Edouard Michelin.

BASIC VALUES

France is in sore need of corporate champions these days. The youthful, successful Gallic CEO, as epitomized by Vivendi Universal's flamboyant Jean-Marie Messier, is looking more and more like a fallen idol—a victim of overweening pride, cratering stock valuations, and the now-discredited cult of the dot-com.

Those individuals who are seeking to repair their broken faith in the French business Establishment should consider a pilgrimage to Clermont-Ferrand, a small town in southern France. There they will find Edouard Michelin, the CEO and scion of the French tire company that bears his name. With a nearly 20 percent share of the global $70 billion tire market, Michelin is the world's top tiremaker—a title that it recently reclaimed from Japan's Bridgestone Corp. On the surface, Michelin looks like the very antithesis of a New Economy company: it's 113 years old, it's family-run, and it makes . . . well, tires. It also, wonder of wonders, makes money—operating profits are expected to hit $1.06 billion in 2002, a 7 percent jump from last year and a strong performance in a soft global economy. "Two years ago, companies were valued on the basis of things like 'return on clicks,'" says Edouard Michelin. "Today, we're all coming back to basic values."

In some ways, the fourth-generation Michelin is as conservative as they come. At 39, Edouard Michelin ranks as one of Europe's youngest bosses. A family man with six children, Edouard leads a modest lifestyle: no yacht, no jets, no $17.5 million Park Avenue apartment. His one weakness: fast cars. Parked in Edouard's driveway is a $63,000, 380-horsepower, limited-edition Audi RS4.

MORE FLASH FROM MICHELIN

That Audi gives a hint that the auto industry may expect a little more flash from Michelin—especially now, the year when Michelin's CEO has finally emerged from his father's shadow. Although Edouard has run the company since 1999, when his father, François, handed over the reins, François stayed on as managing partner until May, when he relinquished that post at the age of 75. During his 44 years at the helm, the elder Michelin acquired a reputation as an iron-fisted boss, but he also transformed the provincial tiremaker into a global leader. Today, three giants—Michelin, Bridgestone, and Goodyear—

have nearly 60 percent of the global tire market, followed by Germany's Continental and Italy's Pirelli.

QUALITY FOCUS IN PRICE CONSCIOUS MARKET

Edouard has been with the company since 1989, when he graduated from France's prestigious Ecole Centrale. He still consults with his father regularly, yet it is clear that he is eager to put his own stamp on the company. He's out to make Michelin, with $15.5 billion in annual sales, the undisputed number one tiremaker worldwide, with a comfortable lead over its rivals. And he wants to squeeze a bigger profit out of every single tire that he sells: his goal is to achieve a consistent 10 percent operating margin, something that Michelin has yet to pull off during his tenure. Wide margins are hard to come by in an industry whose dynamics are so hostile to profits. The investment needed to make state-of-the-art tires is huge. And Michelin, along with its rivals, is under huge pressure from customers, notably automakers, to keep prices low. Just as menacing, the basic quality of a commodity tire is pretty good—good enough so that many consumers still buy on price despite greater concerns about safety.

Edouard is battling that trend with technologically advanced products that offer superior performance and command a premium. Take the PAX "run flat" tire, which Michelin will be showcasing at the upcoming Paris auto show. With a starting price of $140, the PAX can go 200 km after it has been punctured. Michelin's managers say that the emphasis on top-end products has helped reverse a two-year slide in earnings: the company reported a 16 percent jump in operating profit in the first half of 2002, to $540 million. And the stock is up 26 percent in the last 12 months.

Edouard is also opening up the company—once one of the most secretive in Europe—to make it more responsive to its customers and shareholders. He allows top auto executives sneak peeks at projects inside the closely guarded research facilities at Ladoux to involve them during the earliest stages of the design process. He meets with investors every two to three weeks, the first Michelin boss to do so. The company even welcomed analysts into its Clermont-Ferrand plant and gave them a crash course in tire manufacturing. Michelin's once-chilly relations with French unions also have warmed. "Edouard

POWER MOVE

Today, not even a century-old family business can maintain intense insularity. Frequent interactions with customers and critics allow Michelin to test new product and marketing concepts, gather useful feedback, and—just as importantly—build trust.

is more willing to negotiate," says Hervé Carrusca, the local representative of the Force Ouvrière union. "Before, with his father, there were no discussions."

Edouard, who honed his talents during a three-year stint at Michelin's U.S. headquarters in Greenville, South Carolina, is also streamlining management to push for greater accountability and has reached out to employees with a popular stock-option plan. "Edouard is bringing an Anglo-Saxon touch in several areas, notably in terms of relations with outside shareholders and management techniques. He clearly has his own ideas," says Louis Schweitzer, CEO of French automaker Renault.

BUILD TRUST WITH CONSUMER FEEDBACK

In his quest for global leadership, Michelin has a valuable helpmate: the Michelin Man, who goes by the name of Bibendum in France and Bi-bi-deng in China. "No other tire company has anything like him," says Steve Saxty, executive director of automotive practice at FutureBrand Co., a New York consulting firm. You may not have noticed, but Michelin's 104-year-old mascot now sports a more muscular silhouette, the result of some discreet liposuction.

The question now is how fit Edouard can make his company. Michelin is already more profitable than Goodyear and Bridgestone, which was hammered by a tire recall at its U.S. Firestone unit two years ago. Still, Michelin's operating margins, now at 7 percent, have seesawed over the past decade. Investors will punish Michelin if he doesn't hit his avowed goal of 10 percent.

That's why innovation is critical. Michelin plows 4 percent of sales back into research and development, outspending its rivals (with the possible exception of Bridgestone, which doesn't disclose figures). The research pays off in aerospace, too. When the Concorde resumed flights last November, the supersonic jet was outfitted with new Michelin tires specially designed to resist the kind of puncture that burst one of the plane's Goodyear tires two years ago in Paris, leading to a deadly crash. Michelin is also the exclusive supplier to the U.S.

Space Shuttle program. "With Michelin's technology, we feel we're uniquely positioned, if we don't make mistakes, to be the undisputed leader," says Edouard.

That's a bold claim, and one that's about to be tested. The company that brought you the radial tire in 1946 is now busy promoting the PAX as the industry's first "run flat" tire. Bridgestone has rushed out its own version of the PAX, priced around one-third less, but carmakers are willing to pay a premium for Michelin's patented technology. The PAX's gel-filled interior ring ensures such a smooth ride that drivers often don't know that they've gotten a flat. They're alerted by a pressure-monitoring system that tells them that the tire has been punctured and to reduce speed to 50 mph (80 km per hour). The PAX, already available on Renault's Scenic minivans, will be offered as an option on Audi's top-of-the-line $66,000 A8 sedan due out this fall and on Cadillac's upcoming luxury roadster.

FOCUS ON MOST PROFITABLE CUSTOMERS
Meanwhile, Edouard is backing off from customers that deliver volume but little profit. In May, Michelin dumped long-standing customers GM Europe and Fiat to concentrate on the premium end of the business. That means selling more tires like the $398, 20-inch Diamaris that BMW fits on its popular X5 SUV. "What Michelin seems to be doing is not pursuing contracts at any price," says BMW CEO Helmut Panke.

High-performance tires like the Diamaris command price premiums twice or more those of regular tires, while sales in this segment are growing by 10 percent a year, compared with 2 percent for the overall tire market. Premium tires now make up 44 percent of the French company's total car tire sales, up from 30 percent in 1998.

CAPITALIZE ON COMPETITOR'S MISSTEPS
In the United States, heightened brand awareness in the wake of the Firestone recall has enabled Michelin to boost market share even though it has jacked up prices by up to 6 percent in the past year. "We've seen a clear change in the behavior of the American consumer, with people inquiring much more before buying a tire," says Edouard. After Ford Motor Co. blamed deadly SUV blowouts on Firestone tires two years ago, Michelin's long-standing ad campaign—with its tag line "because so much is riding on your

tires"—resonated with customers. "I think it's significant that their advertising emphasizes safety," says Scot Bernstein, a Sacramento (California)-based securities attorney who has Michelin all-terrain tires on his Jeep and all-weather Michelins on his cherished 1978 Camaro. Jerry Nerheim, president of Waukegan Tire & Supply Inc. in Waukegan, Illinois, says that Michelin tires are his biggest sellers. "Michelin is what everybody shoots at—to be as good as them. They set the standards," he says.

Since the Firestone debacle, Michelin's share of the U.S. tire market—which includes its American brands B.F. Goodrich and Uniroyal—has risen three points, to 25 percent. "They're raising prices [in the United States and Europe] and gaining market share," says Patrice Solaro, an analyst at Julius Baer in Paris. "But how long does that last?"

MAINTAIN POSITION WITH SUPERIOR SERVICE

Edouard believes that he can lock in his gains with superior service. The equipment used in the new C3M tiremaking process is so compact that it can be shipped from one facility to another in just one planeload. Yet it performs the same functions as a traditional factory. Michelin executives say that the process, implemented in 2001, gives them the flexibility to produce small batches of premium tires rapidly without tying up regular production lines. "It's a very valuable tool for us," says an executive at one European auto company that has used the technology. Challengers Pirelli and Goodyear have since developed similar versions of C3M.

For all his smart moves of late, Edouard got off to a clumsy start as CEO. Three months after being elevated to the post in June 1999, he sparked demonstrations and a rebuke from the French government by announcing cuts of 7,500 jobs the same day that Michelin reported a big rise in earnings. But he learned fast. When the previous Socialist government mandated a

POWER MOVE

In France, a nation with such a particular employment culture that even a Frenchman can stumble, multinational executives must tread carefully when introducing modern management techniques. As globalization continues, it will be increasingly important to take local customs and traditions into account—even if all business transactions occur in English.

cut in the workweek to 35 hours, Edouard agreed to negotiate with Michelin's unions, marking a break with his father's take-it-or-leave-it stance. "What people like about Edouard is that he's honest and he learns from his mistakes," says Noel Goutard, retired CEO and now supervisory board honorary chairman of auto parts supplier Valeo.

Although more mellow than his father, Edouard has still proved to be an aggressive cost cutter. On top of the recently completed layoffs in Europe, he has kicked off a $100 million restructuring plan that will eliminate 2,000 jobs at Michelin's operations throughout the United States over the course of this year and the next, yielding $200 million a year in savings.

Edouard is also pursuing the aggressive global strategy that his father started. On a trip to China in mid-July, he dropped in unannounced on a truck tire dealer in the province of Szechwan. Why, Michelin wanted to know, are sales of radial tires surging in China even though they cost three times more than standard tires? As local Michelin staff translated, the dealer explained that Chinese haulers routinely overload their trucks, packing 20 tons on vehicles built to carry 5. The result? After a few trips, the tires burst. But steel-reinforced radials can take the beating.

They sure do. Michelin became number one in China last year, with a 30 percent share of the replacement tire market, after signing a deal to pump $143 million over three years into a majority-owned joint venture with the Shanghai Tire & Rubber Co. "Whoever is number one in China and can hold on to that will be number one in Asia in 30 years," predicts Hervé Coyco, head of the car and light truck tire division. Beware, Bridgestone; Bi-bi-deng is flexing his muscles.

UPDATE

Tragically, Edouard Michelin died in the shipwreck of a fishing boat off the French coast in May 2006. His untimely death was taken especially hard by the French business and political communities, who saw him as one of the nation's great leaders. Michael Rollier, who had previously shared the CEO title with Michelin, later announced his intention to follow the strategy that Michelin had developed.

MONDAY MORNING...

THE PROBLEM

Maintaining your premium product strategy in a price-sensitive industry

Avoiding the backlash from a competitor's unfortunate disaster

THE SOLUTION

Differentiate your company with positioning that highlights your technological superiority.

Update antiquated management practices within the national context.

SUSTAINING THE WIN

Invest heavily in R&D.

Get into emerging markets early to learn from joint ventures, but watch out for increasingly sophisticated homegrown competitors.

KEN CHENAULT: CHARGE! AT AMERICAN EXPRESS

©Nigel Parry / CPI

POWER PLAYER

Kenneth Chenault has made history as the first African American to head one of the 30 Dow Jones Industrial Average companies—financial services powerhouse American Express. He shaken up the credit card industry by moving into territory long dominated by Visa and MasterCard.

This story from 2004 by Mara Der Hovanesian looks at Ken Chenault as he is about to launch a huge credit card war.

SEIZE THE MOMENT

This is the moment that Kenneth I. Chenault, chief executive of American Express Co. , has been waiting for throughout his entire career. As a fresh recruit in charge of strategic planning more than two decades ago, he sought to move AmEx beyond its lucrative niche as an upscale charge card—an idea that was too radical for the company's old guard. Later, as head of consumer cards, he began a dogged campaign against industry giants Visa USA Inc. and MasterCard International Inc. and the lock they have on issuing cards through banks. "I've had a willingness to take on conventional views, to shake things up," says the 53-year-old Chenault.

Willingness is one thing, opportunity another. But now Chenault has both. This fall, the U.S. Supreme Court is expected to uphold a ruling by the U.S. District Court for the Southern District of New York that Visa and MasterCard—which together control 79 percent of the U.S. card market—stifle competition and innovation by forbidding the banks that own them from issuing rival cards. For the first time in its 154-year history, AmEx will have carte blanche to issue plastic through U.S. banks and flood the market with millions of its green, gold, and platinum cards. The ruling, the culmination of an antitrust case launched by the Department of Justice six years ago, "will create competition in our industry for the first time," says David W. Nelms, chairman and CEO of Morgan Stanley's Discover Financial Services Inc. unit.

SOUPED-UP REWARDS PROGRAMS

The Supreme Court's decision—and Chenault's plans to exploit it aggressively—would change the $2.1 trillion card business for good. Already, the industry is in the midst of the biggest fight in its history for share of a saturated market. All the major brands and banks are in a frenzy to woo fickle high spenders. Their weapon of choice: souped-up rewards programs, a marketing tool that AmEx pioneered. AmEx now gives big cash rebates and mileage points redeemable for space travel. U.S. Bancorp offers private yoga lessons with actress Gwyneth Paltrow on its new Stratus Rewards Visa cards. And in the hunt for more outlets, once-exclusive cards such as Citigroup's Diner's Club will soon be accepted in Wendy's as well as the Waldorf-Astoria. Says John C. Grund, partner with First Annapolis Consulting Inc., a Maryland-based industry specialist: "It's now a matter of how to steal share from one another, innovate, and tap new markets."

SEIZE THE OPPORTUNITY

This free-for-all is ushering in the long-predicted cashless society. Uncle Sam takes plastic; welfare benefits and salaries are paid by loading a card with cash. Yet American consumers still use cash or checks to pay for about 59 percent of the $8.2 trillion a year they spend on everything from housing to hamburgers. If the card industry can capture even a modest part of those $4.8 trillion cash outlays, it will experience fast growth. *The Nilson Report*, an industry newsletter, forecasts that combined debit and credit card spending will grow 13 percent a year through 2007. "You're talking about the most profitable retail banking product in the world. The competition among the titans is going to be fierce," says *Nilson* publisher David Robertson. "They are already clobbering each other."

The slugfest seems certain to whack the card companies' margins, which are under legal attack by merchants and regulators. AmEx has the most to lose. It charges merchants about 2.6 percent of customers' bills, more than the roughly 2 percent levied by Visa and MasterCard. Indeed, AmEx's average fee fell by 2.3 percent last year, according to company filings. Traditionally, card companies have been loath to negotiate on fees. But some merchants are being so ardently courted that they're able to bargain. In April, Costco Wholesale Corp. the nation's number one warehouse retailer, signed a 10-year exclusive contract with AmEx because it got better (but undisclosed) terms than rivals would offer. "Visa and MasterCard's fees are outrageous," says Costco CEO James D. Sinegal. "Neither gave us any wiggle room."

MORE CASH FROM MORE CUSTOMERS

With his margins under pressure, Chenault must drive up the amount that consumers spend using his cards. He's doing just that; in the second quarter of this year, such spending leapt 19 percent, topping $100 billion for the first time. His strategy is simple: first, he wants to get more cards in people's hands by persuading banks to switch customers from Visa and MasterCard to AmEx. Then he aims to coax cardholders to spend more—and buy other AmEx products.

Extending the AmEx brand will help the company acquire customers, who will buy other AmEx products and enjoy the benefits of single sourcing, such as integrated online account management. With more accurate data on its customers' preferences, AmEx will provide increasingly tailored offerings, giving customers even more reason to stay.

AmEx isn't looking to snag just any customers from Visa and MasterCard. It wants the affluent investor class, those who earn between $100,000 and $1 million a year. These people charge a bundle, keeping the card's profile high, and pay off their balances in full. With thousands of new big spenders in the fold, Chenault's battalion of 12,000 financial advisers would move in to sell them advice and financial plans, which start at $500 a pop. Then they'll sell insurance and investment products, including AmEx's own.

"We have to be the number one provider to high-spending customers for both cards and financial advice," says Chenault. "We will have an advantage because we have a very clear focus on these customers."

At the same time, AmEx will step up its drive to wean large companies and small businesses from checks to corporate plastic. Analysts figure that a $400 billion a year U.S. market for procurement and payroll is up for grabs. And, although AmEx is five times bigger than its nearest competitor in providing commercial cards to owners of small businesses, Chenault is chasing after a bigger share of their $4 trillion worth of spending. Just $90 billion of those outlays are made with credit cards.

AIM FOR THE HIGH END

Even before AmEx issues its first card through a U.S. bank, competitors are fighting back. They are promoting heavily gold and platinum cards aimed at AmEx's high-end customers. In mid-July, Visa launched a media blitz for its redesigned Signature Card, through which customers spent $80 billion last year. MasterCard is revamping its World MasterCard. Brokerages and banks are wading in, too. "A lot of cards don't completely meet the needs or desires of the upper class," says Christopher L. Pieroth, senior vice president of product and marketing for U.S. Bancorp of Minneapolis, the eighth-largest U.S. bank, which launched its Stratus Rewards Card in April. Cardholders can accumulate points toward private tours of the

Louvre and the Egyptian Pyramids, as well as private jet travel. "The players are recognizing this is a very lucrative market; you are going to see a big push."

Chenault is betting that the high status of AmEx's cards can help him grab a good chunk of future market growth. The key is to make his cards stand out among the 848 million cards circulating in the United States today. Last year, some 8,000 card issuers mailed five billion solicitations—40 per household. The response rate has plunged. Instead of adding cards to their wallet, people are now replacing the ones they already have, says John Gould, a director at Tower Group, a Needham (Massachusetts) financial consultancy. And that, he says, should open the door for AmEx: "They are creative. They have something of interest to the issuers that Visa and MasterCard do not—prestige."

ECONOMIES OF SCALE

AmEx has more to offer than just prestige. Because it charges merchants about half a percentage point more than Visa and MasterCard, it can afford to give banks a bigger slice of its fees. The mix appealed to MBNA, the first bank to strike a deal to issue AmEx-branded cards as early as the end of this year. That was quite a coup for Chenault. MBNA issues more MasterCards and Visas—some 56 million altogether—than any other bank. "You generally don't like helping your competitors, but sometimes it makes sense," says MBNA Chief Executive Bruce Hammonds. "We are both able to make more money and expand our business." McLean (Virginia)-based Capital One Financial Corp., another big customer of the giants, could be the next convert, say analysts. (Capital One declined to comment.) Meantime, Chenault is courting dozens of banks that he thinks will sign on if the courts outlaw Visa's and MasterCard's restrictive contracts.

Chenault's gamble could pay off big on AmEx's bottom line. For one thing, the banks issuing AmEx cards will bear the cost if customers don't pay their bills, something that AmEx shoulders on its own cards. And with more cards in circulation, Chenault should be able to extract significant economies of scale from AmEx's network linking merchants, banks, and customers. "More cards will be issued, more merchants will choose to take the card, and the economics of the entire firm start to lift," says Howard K. Mason, a senior bank analyst with Sanford C. Bernstein & Co. For each 10 percent rise in card billings, he figures, AmEx will incur just 1.5 percent more in network costs. So AmEx's current 20 percent return on equity should get a big boost. Adds Richard Freeman, a management professor at New York University's Stern School of Business: "If they get access to the bank business, I think there is a huge potential upside."

DON'T DILUTE THE BRAND

First, though, Chenault has to pull off some fancy footwork. His trickiest maneuver will be to recruit millions more cardholders without diluting AmEx's gold-standard brand. According to the *BusinessWeek*/Interbrand 2004 ranking, it was the fourteenth most valuable brand in the world, worth nearly $18 billion. What's more, AmEx won't have debit cards, which are growing 17 percent a year— twice as fast as credit cards—until Chenault sets up a system to link them with bank accounts. And the money-management business is still recovering from years of missteps. For the last three years, less than one-fifth of AmEx's 72 retail equity mutual funds ranked in the top quartile of their peer group, according to fund tracker Lipper Inc.

POWER MOVE

Maintaining its prestige will be challenging, but the expansion also offers AmEx the opportunity to shed any unwanted perceptions—such as stuffy, expensive, or elitist—that might previously have tainted its identity.

In fact, Chenault has to juggle several problems simultaneously if he is to achieve his goal of dominating the high end of both the card and financial-advice businesses. He has to gain market share without allowing AmEx's margins to shrink too much. He has to coax enough extra merchants to accept his card and pay his higher fees. And he has to persuade banks to let him offer AmEx's financial services alongside their own. "Who owns the consumer?" asks William H. McCracken, chief executive of the consumer market researcher Synergistics Research Corp. in Atlanta. "Is it the issuing bank, or American Express, or both? If it's both, that raises some thorny questions."

For now, banks seem attracted by AmEx's willingness to pay them more. But Chenault's main rivals are trying to close the gap. In April, they raised their merchant fees on credit cards by about 5 percent, so they can pay banks more, according to *Nilson*. Critics say that the ploy is bound to backfire. "If the strategy is to help banks reach more into merchants' pockets, that's a dangerous prospect," says Kenneth A. Posner, credit card analyst for Morgan Stanley, who figures that half of the $24 billion a year they already earn from such fees could be at risk.

Merchants are already upset. Last year, they wrestled a $3 billion settlement (to be paid over 10 years) from Visa and MasterCard in an antitrust class action, led by Wal-Mart Stores Inc. The suit alleged that the card groups strong-armed merchants into paying high fees for debit card transactions, which the groups denied. Some big merchants that opted out of the class action, including Home Depot (HD), are still seeking damages in other suits. Discover, for one, sees an opportunity. "We could be the solution for angry merchants," says Discover's Nelms. Merchants pay up to 15 percent less on average to Discover than to Visa and MasterCard, according to *The Nilson Report*. "We obviously are taking to heart the lessons," adds Robert W. Selander, president and CEO of MasterCard. "If you settle for a billion dollars, obviously, you do more than just write some checks." Bottom line: MasterCard is ready to haggle with big merchants.

EARN THE TRUST OF YOUR DETRACTORS

AmEx is facing a challenge over its own fees. Last August, attorney Blaine H. Bortnick of New York's Liddle & Robinson and Gary B. Friedman of Friedman & Shube filed an antitrust suit on behalf of several small merchants, alleging that AmEx charges excessive fees. "The Wal-Mart case was part of the inspiration," says Bortnick, who is trying to gain class action status for the suit. AmEx says it will fight such cases vigorously.

Such suits would appear to be a major headache for Chenault. AmEx gets about 65 percent of its card revenues from merchant fees, while Visa and MasterCard generate only about 20 percent of their revenues from their share of the merchant fees. That's because its rivals rely on interest on outstanding balances, while AmEx depends on high levels of spending. Chenault expects to sacrifice some of his margins to grasp the opportunity presented by unfettered competition. He believes that by cherry-picking banks and merchants, he can increase not only the number of transactions on his card, but also the amount spent on each. Says Chenault: "I'm not complacent or unaware of the pressures. The burden on us is that we have to deliver value for the premium price."

What the merchants value most is the number of high-spending clients that Chenault can deliver. AmEx customers are attractive because they use their cards more often than those of rivals and spend an average of more than $8,000 a year—about twice as much as Visa and MasterCard users. Still, Chenault is playing catch-up with Visa and MasterCard. They each have 5.2 million merchants on their rosters, vs. 3.5 million for AmEx. "We're everywhere AmEx wants to be," quips Tim Attinger, a senior Visa executive.

By some measures, that's streets ahead of AmEx. Visa's 430 million cards account for $1.1 trillion in spending in the United States whereas AmEx's 35 million cards account for $260 billion in charges. Visa's everyday spending category is growing about $100 billion a year, or 5.5 percent, primarily thanks to debit cards. "AmEx is a niche player today and is going to be even more so because of the explosive growth that's coming in prepaid and debit," says Elizabeth Buse, executive vice president for product development at Visa.

Chenault aims to close the gaps by launching new products and rewards programs galore to entice customers to spend more. AmEx's Blue card—aimed at capturing everyday spending on items from groceries to dry cleaning and postage stamps—now offers up to 5 percent cash rebates and double bonus points. New prepaid cards loaded with cash, which AmEx may customize for big-ticket events such as weddings and bar mitzvahs, are designed to tap a market worth some $105 billion. And it's testing ExpressPay, a payment device linked to its cards and activated by radio, at more than 600 locations, including chains Eckerd Drugs, Blimpie Subs & Salads, and Carl's Jr. And AmEx is pushing hard to get charge cards accepted by landlords and cash-and-carry wholesale suppliers. Last year, for example, it teamed up with New York's Related Cos. to allow tenants to pay their rent with plastic at 16 luxury buildings.

CHOOSE WELL YOUR PARTNERS

Because Chenault's whole strategy hinges on his ability to keep his cardholders spending big, he will be picky about which banks he signs up. Their customers will have to spend enough to maintain AmEx's averages. He also insists that the banks use some of the extra money they earn from him to develop their own customized rewards programs. If banks don't deliver, "we absolutely pull the plug," says Chenault. That's no idle threat: Chenault ended a card deal with

Canadian Imperial Bank of Commerce by mutual agreement in June after just 18 months. "The cards were not meeting our financial objectives," says CIBC spokeswoman Susan McDougall.

Critics contend that such tough conditions could deter some banks from issuing AmEx cards. Chenault counters that he's offering far more than just cards. For a fee, community banks, credit unions, and midsize banks will be able to tap AmEx's expertise in corporate T&E and procurement cards for small business, two areas in which it is a market leader. Some have sold AmEx annuities for years. Chenault says he can help banks do a better job selling investments and advice to the affluent. Banks account for about 17 percent of $180 billion in annual mutual-fund sales and 1 percent of $480 billion in life insurance sales, according to Celent Communications LLC. Says U.S. Bancorp's Pieroth: "Banks are probably not the most creative when it comes to targeting niche markets." Indeed, banks are way behind brokers, who have captured nearly two-thirds of the sales of investments to high-net-worth customers.

SPURRING INVESTMENT

AmEx needs new outlets to sell its financial planning services—and banks offer a tempting prospect. The more plans Chenault sells, the more likely it is that he'll sell other products: last year, financial plans sold by AmEx advisers led to three-quarters of the $1.4 billion of mostly retail sales by the company's Minneapolis-based American Express Financial Advisors Inc. unit. If banks bristle at the idea of AmEx's advisers selling to their customers, Chenault won't insist—though he thinks they would be making a mistake. "Customer needs and competitor pressures [are opening] up the system," he says.

He is also pushing large companies that offer AmEx funds in their 401(k) retirement plans to host investment seminars. Such programs accounted for about 18 percent of AmEx's new clients last year. And he has placed advisers in more than 300 Costcos nationwide. Existing cardmembers have yet

POWER MOVE

In 2005, the AEFA unit was spun off and renamed Ameriprise Financial Inc., allowing the remaining AmEx businesses to focus on their credit card and travel service businesses. Though Ameriprise has given up the prestige of its former corporate parent, its newly found freedom allows it to raise money more quickly—outside of the AmEx walls.

to be tapped for their full potential, says James M. Cracchiolo, AEFA's chief executive. He figures that they have about $80 billion in cash and investments at banks and brokerages that he would like to consolidate at AmEx.

Financial plans may be an easier sell than AmEx's investment products. Since he became CEO, however, Chenault has shuffled AEFA's executive management, hired new money managers, and added a new lineup of products for retail and institutional investors. New lines such as the AXP Partners funds, managed by top-notch firms such as Gabelli Asset Management Inc. and Wellington Management Co., have performed better than AmEx's in-house funds, averaging a one-year return of 14 percent, vs. 8 percent for the in-house funds. Better yet, they've attracted $4.8 billion from retail investors since January 2001. The result: AEFA revenues rose 18 percent in the second quarter, and assets grew 55 percent to $380 billion over the past year.

Skeptics doubt whether Chenault can snare big outfits such as Citigroup, which is busy building its own credit card brand and financial-services business. Citi's chief operating officer and president, Robert B. Willumstad, told analysts in February that a partnership with AmEx was unlikely, although executives from the two companies have met. Besides, Citi put its high-end, but languishing, Diner's Club (the first charge card on the market, started in 1950) in direct competition with AmEx by partnering with MasterCard in April. However, Bernstein's Mason figures that Citi may relent, if only to give its customers a choice. "Attrition is a nasty thing," he says. "Citi and others must factor in the cost of not doing business with AmEx." Adds MasterCard's Selander: "It's certainly not going to be an exodus; my guess is it will be more of an experiment."

BRING GLOBAL LESSONS HOME

Whatever obstacles Chenault faces in the United States, he knows that his strategy has been road-tested abroad. And it worked. Wherever AmEx has been free to sign up banks, competition for cards and financial services has thrived. Since its launch in 1999, AmEx's global network services, one of its fastest-growing divisions, has signed up 84 banks in 94 countries. Last year, its billings topped $12 billion; spending jumped 30 percent in the second quarter.

In his three years as head of AmEx, Chenault has faced several severe tests. Four months after he became CEO in January 2001, the company was rocked by revelations of a $1 billion loss on a junk-bond bet gone bad. Then, September 11 not only dislodged AmEx from its Lower Manhattan headquarters, but also stopped the company's core corporate travel and entertainment business in its tracks. Profits halved and AmEx's future looked so bleak that rumors flew around Wall Street that it might soon be snapped up by the likes of Citigroup. "Anything that could have been thrown at us was," says Chenault.

He soon regained the initiative. He swallowed the $1 billion loss on junk bonds and cut risky corporate lending in half. As business disappeared in the wake of September 11, he slashed 14,500 jobs, 16 percent of the workforce, and outsourced 2,000 tech jobs to IBM. By the end of this year, he will have shaved a cumulative $4 billion off costs. "Investors were doubtful that the company could recover," says analyst David A. Hendler of CreditSights Ltd. "Chenault has done an awesome job."

It was a job of building as well as cutting. While other CEOs hunkered down during the recession, Chenault bought two companies—AmEx's first sizable acquisitions in more than a decade. Since 2002, he has pumped $7.8 billion into marketing, promotion, and rewards programs—almost 12.2 percent of revenues. Bolder still, he turned AmEx's business model on its head. Before September 11, two-thirds of its card billings came from corporate T&E and a third from regular consumer spending. By last year, the ratios were reversed. "We are engaged in a very important transformation for this company," says Chenault. "American Express is a new story."

It's a story with a big payday, at that. On July 26, AmEx reported record profits of $876 million and record revenues of $7.3 billion for the second quarter. Says former

POWER MOVE

Business history is littered with stories about companies that failed to adjust during downturns—Silicon Valley's Sun Microsystems, for example. To avoid such a debacle, Chenault cut thousands of positions, especially in travel services. But he also took enough of a long-term view to make smart acquisitions that would later prove critical.

IBM Chairman Louis V. Gerstner Jr., who ran AmEx for 11 years and recruited Chenault from consultants Bain & Co. in 1981: "Once he figures out what he needs to do, he has the drive to take the risk and to make it happen. He is a superb problem-solver."

The solution to his latest challenges lies in the hands of consumers. His competitors won't surrender ground without a struggle, but Chenault believes that their customers will switch to his card when they get the chance. As he tells bankers he's now trying to sign up: "Change is in the cards." It surely will be if the Supreme Court changes the rules of the game.

THE PROBLEM
Developing new products and services that extend the appeal of a premium brand—without losing its prestige

Winning in a highly competitive, cluttered marketplace

THE SOLUTION
Partner only with companies that can deliver customers, brands, and benefits that meet your premium standards.

Develop creative product and service offerings, such as the IN:NYC, IN:Chicago, and IN:LA Cards, aligned with your image of exclusivity.

SUSTAINING THE WIN
Invest heavily in maintaining your brand identity.

BUSINESS PROPHET
C. K. PRAHALAD IS CHANGING
THE WAY CEOS THINK

Take a cab ride through Bombay, and these are the scenes that are likely to strike you first: raggedly dressed homeless families sprawled on blankets amid shacks; traffic hopelessly clogged with every manner of soot-belching vehicle and wooden cart; gaunt hawkers and beggars tapping on your window at red lights. For foreign visitors, such jarring images of poverty and desperation are hard to shake.

When you view those same streets through the eyes of C. K. Prahalad, however, they become a beehive of entrepreneurialism and creativity. "I see the positives inside the muck," says Prahalad as he settles his stocky frame into the back of a hired Tata Indica sedan to conduct a quick tour of Bombay. As the car crawls through congested Mohamed Ali Road, he notes that virtually every individual is engaged in a business of some kind—whether it is selling single cloves of garlic, squeezing sugar cane juice for pennies a glass, or hauling TVs.

On every block, he points out the intriguing enterprises tucked into the nooks and crannies. With the world's cheapest telecom rates, "all you need here is a phone and a $20 card to start a business," he explains in his measured baritone. He notices a busy closet-sized shop charging a few pennies per page to send faxes. "That guy probably started with a single phone and then added a fax and printer. Now he has a self-contained communications center offering extremely low prices." Such entrepreneurs, he contends, pioneered cheap pay-per-use services long before they became a fad in the West. The car stops at a small dry-goods shop. Prahalad bounds out and asks the owner to let him behind the counter. Tiny five-cent single-serving containers of shampoo, soap, toothpaste, and other household goods dangle from the walls and ceiling. He notes the

POWER PLAY

Think big. Set ambitious goals and then figure out how to mobilize the resources to achieve them—rather than the other way around.

brands: Head & Shoulders, Lifebuoy, Pears, Colgate, Lux. "Low quality won't sell," he says.

After an hour of this, it's hard to look at Bombay and its impoverished citizens in the same way. That's exactly what Prahalad, 64, intended. The University of Michigan professor's knack for being able to change people's perceptions of the world around them has made Prahalad an incredibly influential corporate strategist. He has built a lucrative consulting career helping such multinationals as Citibank, Philips, and Philip Morris break out of ingrained mindsets and craft new business models. Prahalad and colleague Gary Hamel helped spark a management revolution in the 1990s with their idea of "core competence," which states that companies must identify and focus on their competitive strengths. Their 1994 book, *Competing for the Future*, is regarded as a classic. A decade later, Prahalad co-wrote *The Future of Competition*, which argued that the traditional "company-centric" approach to product innovation is giving way to a world in which companies "co-create" products with consumers. That book gave Prahalad a reputation among designers. At the same time, he has been working to convince executives that today's needy masses, so often dismissed as subsisting largely outside of the global economy, are actually its future. Prahalad's 2004 work on that topic, *The Fortune at the Bottom of the Pyramid*, has been hailed as one of the most important business books in recent years and has turned Prahalad into a celebrity in the field of international development.

STREET-SMART INNOVATION

Now one of the management world's most creative thinkers has an even more radical idea: he believes that the entrepreneurial ingenuity at work amid such poverty, where success depends on squeezing the most out of minimal resources to furnish quality products at rock-bottom prices, has cosmic implications for executives and consumers everywhere. "Some of the most interesting companies of the future won't emerge from Silicon Valley or other places of abundant means," he says. "They will come from places that many executives don't even think about because they are considered too marginal. Those executives won't have that excuse for much longer, though."

In the world according to C. K. (short for Coimbatore Krishnarao), poor nations are incubating new business models and innovative uses of technology that in the coming decade will begin to transform the competitive landscape of entire global industries, from financial and telecommunications services to health care and carmaking. Globalization, outsourcing, the Internet, and the spread of cheap wireless telecommunications are accelerating dramatic change. Few Western corporations are fully harnessing these forces, Prahalad warns. And that puts them in danger of being usurped by a new breed of supercompetitive multinationals that are completely off their radar screens, just as American industrial icons such as Xerox, General Motors, and RCA were blindsided in the 1970s and 1980s by nimbler Japanese upstarts, such as Canon, Toyota, and Sony.

For his next book, due in the fall of 2006, Prahalad is assembling case studies of Indian companies that could spawn entirely new ways to think about conducting business. Fast-growing telecommunications operators such as Bharti, Reliance, and Tata, for example, are profitably selling cellular service for as little as two cents a minute, "even though they must buy the same hardware as Western companies," he says. Now they're preparing to launch broadband TV, data, and voice packages for around $30 a month—about a third the cost of such packages in the United States. Bangalore's Narayana Hrudayalaya hospital charges a flat fee of only $1,500 for heart bypass surgery that would cost 50 times that in the United States and operates on hundreds of infants each year for free. Yet it is highly profitable, has no debt, and claims a higher success rate than most U.S. hospitals. Narayana also profitably insures 2.5 million poor Indians against serious illness for 11 cents a month per person.

Low wages alone can't account for such price gaps with the West, Prahalad contends. The real secret is ingenious cost-cutting practices, such as extreme reliance on outsourcing, novel use of technology, and making the most of capital investment. "These are radical innovations," Prahalad says, many of which can be adapted to the United States. Just look at the information

POWER PLAY

Cater to the poor. People living in poverty, both in the United States and abroad, can be immensely important markets for consumer goods, telecommunications, and financial services. But they require high-quality products at lower prices.

technology industry: long dominated by giants IBM, EDS, and Accenture, it has already been transformed by Indian companies such as Infosys and Wipro that supply top-quality services at lower prices. That, says Prahalad, is just the beginning of the revolution.

How seriously should we take Prahalad? His theories naturally draw skeptics. For instance, bottom-of-the-pyramid efforts don't always help the bottom line, notes Microsoft Corp. Chief Technology Officer Craig J. Mundie. Prahalad's work has reinforced Microsoft's view that it must develop software for developing nations using different pricing, payment systems, and technologies. "But even if you can execute a plan to sell to the poor, it's not clear you can make money," Mundie says. "Many companies in many industries have struggled to make a go of it, frankly." In response, Prahalad notes that many once argued that a sub-$500 PC was impossible. Now PCs cost as little as $100.

Prahalad hasn't always had the Midas touch himself. A San Diego software firm that he co-founded in 2000 struggled and was eventually sold. Of that experience, Prahalad said that he at least gained some insight into his own management style. "I get extremely energized when there is an extremely complex problem to be solved," he says. "But management is a lot of blocking and tackling."

EVOLVING INSIGHTS

Prahalad has been developing his worldview for decades. Born in India's southern Tamil Nadu province, he acquired his inquisitiveness from his father, a prominent judge who was a voracious scholar of philosophy and literature. At age 19, in between earning a bachelor's degree in physics and a management degree from the Indian Institute of Management, C. K. worked as a manager of a Union Carbide battery plant. Later, while at Harvard Business School, he and classmate Yves L. Doz won attention with their 1975 doctoral thesis on multinationals, one of the first studies to argue that corporations need new structures to project global strategies while adapting to local needs. He also began nurturing concepts that he would build on later in his career: that entrepreneurs should not let limited resources constrain their ambitions or let deeply ingrained biases blind them to revolutionary change.

Prahalad's broad curiosity means that his business insights tend to be fresh and ever-evolving. He consumes tomes on the rise and fall of nations, the spread of languages, and the history of such commodities as salt, tobacco, and cod. He is fascinated by historical maps and bird migration patterns, which offer clues to the world's shifting ecology. Prahalad lives with Gayatri, his wife of 35 years, in a sprawling home in San Diego's posh Rancho Santa Fe district but spends about 40 percent of his time on the road. While traveling, he does his own case studies of new business models and pumps everyone—cab drivers, factory workers, university kitchen staff— for insights. Ask him to tell a joke, though, and he's stumped. "I have to admit, I am not very fun at parties," he admits.

Prahalad built his following among CEOs as a blunt and demanding corporate advisor. Rather than operate with a retinue of junior staff, he likes to arrive alone with his Toshiba laptop, fully armed after doing his own analysis of the company's competitive strengths and weaknesses. He then proposes practical ways to correct management flaws. "The best way to describe C. K. is, he's an out-of-the-box guy who is pragmatic," says Hewlett-Packard Co. CEO Mark V. Hurd, who ran NCR Corp. until March. Prahalad has been on NCR's board since 1997. "It's quite an art to get a board filled with past and current CEOs to think of the world in a different way."

As a consultant, Prahalad begins by trying to force managers to break free from their "dominant logic." The stunt that Prahalad pulled with the top brass of Royal Philips Electronics in 1991 is legendary. The Dutch electronics conglomerate, which was losing market share fast in consumer appliances, hired Prahalad for a weekend brainstorming session. He started the Saturday morning meeting by reading a small item he said he had seen in the *Financial Times*. Philips was heading into bankruptcy, the article speculated, and bankers wanted to know management's game plan. "Forget what we are supposed to talk about. There is a major crisis," Prahalad warned. "You had better figure out what you are going to do about it." He broke the stunned executives into two groups. They returned several hours later with ideas for radical restructuring involving up to 50,000 layoffs. Then Prahalad admitted that he had made the article up.

But he got their attention. Then-CEO Jan Timmer soon launched a restructuring program, with Prahalad supervising a series of meetings with 100 managers from each business unit. "His style was to apply all of the pressure he could," recalls Jan Oosterveld, a retired top executive at Philips who now teaches entrepreneurship at Barcelona's

IESE Business School. "His style can be mean but effective." Philips has since turned itself around through major asset sales, layoffs, better product design, and a keener focus on core technologies.

When Prahalad started working with Indian conglomerates in 1994, "he was so sharp in his criticisms that it was like a punch in the gut," says CEO K. Vaman Kamath of ICICI Bank. "We thought we were leaders. He taught us that Indian banking was a complacent mess and that we would soon be competing with no abilities at all."

Now ICICI exemplifies the kind of company Prahalad sees as the wave of the future. Developing financial software in-house to slash costs, it deployed 2,000 ATMs in urban neighborhoods and villages around the country. Taking a cue from microcredit agencies, ICICI organized thousands of self-help groups that provide loans of as little as $100 to poor women to enable them to start businesses. Today, ICICI ranks as India's dominant consumer bank, having boosted its customer base sevenfold, to 15 million, in six years, while pushing 75 percent of all transactions online. And ICICI's $150 million microcredit business is profitable and expanding fast. ICICI hopes to use its low cost base to expand in Canada and elsewhere.

Prahalad thinks that U.S. financial institutions can learn from ICICI and microlenders in Latin America. "Some 45 million people in this country don't have or don't use bank accounts or ATMs because they are too expensive. So they use check-cashing services, bond brokers, and other alternatives," Prahalad explains. "If the financial industry can bring the poor into the organized sector, there is a tremendous opportunity."

Developing nations are at the forefront of cost reduction in other industries. Among the reasons that Bharti can offer telecommunications service so cheaply, Prahalad says, is that it keeps capital costs down by outsourcing everything from its network infrastructure to its IT systems and promotes the use of prepaid cards that generate cash up front. By making service affordable to the masses, Bharti can lure millions more subscribers, gaining economies of scale, and entice them to rely on cell phones instead of PCs for Internet access. "Somebody will eventually clean up these business models and bring them to the United States," Prahalad predicts. "If high-tech and credit-card companies aren't following these trends, they will get hit."

Prahalad sees big changes ahead in manufacturing as well. GM, Ford, and other automakers are increasingly outsourcing design and computer-simulated parts testing to Indian engineering-services firms. India also is rich in microelectronics design and high-quality precision auto-parts makers specializing in small-batch production. Before long, Prahalad predicts, Indian firms will be creating entire systems for Detroit—such as dashboards and chassis—that will cut development times and costs. "Many companies don't understand yet that outsourcing isn't about exporting jobs. It's about importing innovation," he says.

HEALTHIER HEALTH CARE?

Prahalad thinks that globalization also can help rein in America's soaring health-care costs. That's one reason he is studying Indian hospitals such as Narayana Hrudayalaya, founded by cardiac surgeon Dr. Devi Shetty. Some reasons for its low costs can't be easily replicated elsewhere. The land was owned by Shetty's family. The hospital's 25 foreign-trained surgeons earn half what they could earn in the United States. Outsize malpractice awards are rare in India, so insurance costs are low. But the hospital also operates for free on anyone who cannot pay and on any infant younger than one month. For the rural poor, it runs 39 remote clinics and mobile-testing labs with satellite links that so far have treated 17,000 patients.

POWER PLAY

Reconsider outsourcing. Don't look at it as exporting jobs, but rather as importing innovation. It will allow you to speed up product development, gain new technologies, slash costs, cut capital requirements, and boost flexibility.

Some of the biggest savings come from its business model. In the United States, the chief surgeon manages the entire patient process, from testing and diagnosis to supervising the operating room, recuperation, and billing. Narayana works more like an assembly line: the surgeons perform only surgery.

That may seem like a recipe for shoddy care. But Shetty asserts that it actually translates into fewer mistakes because specialists focus on what they do best. The 1.35 percent mortality rate for coronary bypasses and 2.7 percent rate for aortic valve replacements reported by Narayana are roughly half the average of U.S. hospitals, according to federal statistics, though those aren't the only measures of quality care. "The importance of volume isn't well understood in our industry," Shetty says. "A surgeon doing three or four operations a day does much better work than one doing three or four in a week." The factory approach also leads to economies of scale. The hospital uses all of its expensive CAT scanners and x-ray and magnetic-resonance machines to the max. "In the United States, a lot of this infrastructure is used five days a week," says Shetty. "We use ours 14 hours a day, 7 days a week."

This raises intriguing questions. If Indian doctors can effectively diagnose and treat heart conditions in farmers in distant villages, why can't American consumers use videoconferencing to consult offshore specialists 24/7? Why can't an enterprising hospital chain bring Narayana's model to the United States, or at least set up hospitals in Mexico or the Caribbean charging a fraction of U.S. prices? There are plenty of reasons that this seems unlikely: few Americans would tolerate the inability to collect big damages for mistakes, and it seems far-fetched that the U.S. medical establishment would back sweeping liberalization to license offshore doctors to prescribe treatments. Or does such change seem impossible only because we are blinded by our "dominant logic"? Prahalad is confident that superior business models will eventually prevail. Just gaze into the kaleidoscope, give it a twist, and the implausible in the twenty-first-century global economy becomes more realistic than you might ever imagine.

By Peter Engardio, "Business Prophet," January 23, 2006.

SOURCES

Chapter 1: Tom Lowry, with Amy Barrett and Ronald Grover, "The Cable Guy," November 18, 2002; http://www.businessweek.com/ magazine/content/02_46/b3808001.htm.

Chapter 2: Robert D. Hof, "Reprogramming Amazon," December 22, 2003; http://www.businessweek.com/magazine/content/ 03_51/b3863115_mz063.htm.

Chapter 3: Peter Burrows, "Cisco's Comeback," November 24, 2003; http://www.businessweek.com/magazine/content/03_47/ b3859008.htm.

Chapter 4: Andrew Park, with Peter Burrows, "What You Don't Know about Dell," November 3, 2003; http://www.businessweek. com/magazine/content/03_44/b3856001_ mz001.htm.

Chapter 5: Dean Foust, "Big Brown's New Bag," July 19, 2004; http://www.businessweek.com/magazine/content/04_29/ b3892102_mz017.htm.

Chapter 6: Roger O. Crockett, "Reinventing Motorola," August 2, 2004; http://www.businessweek.com/magazine/content/04_31/ b3894122_mz063.htm.

Chapter 7: Spencer E. Ante, "The New Blue," March 17, 2003; http://www.businessweek.com/magazine/content/03_11/ b3824001_mz001.htm.

Chapter 8: Cliff Edwards, Moon Ihlwan, and Peter Engardio, "The Samsung Way," June 16, 2003; http://www.businessweek. com/magazine/content/03_24/b3837001_mz001.htm.

Chapter 9:   Anthony Bianco, with John Rossant and Lauren Gard, "The Future of the New York Times," January 17, 2005; http://www.businessweek.com/magazine/content/ 05_03/b3916001_mz001.htm.

Chapter 10:   Michael Arndt, "Up from the Scrap Heap," July 21, 2003; http://www.businessweek.com/magazine/content/ 03_29/b3842072.htm.

Chapter 11:   David Welch, David Kiley, and Stanley Holmes, "How Mulally Will Tackle Ford's Troubles," September 07, 2006; http://www.businessweek.com/autos/content/sep2006/ bw20060906_700068.htm.

Chapter 12:   Tom Lowry, "The Prince of Nascar," February 23, 2004; http://www.businessweek.com/magazine/content/ 04_08/b3871101.htm.

Chapter 13:   Christine Tierney, with Ann Therese Palmer, Chester Dawson, and Joann Muller, "Michelin Rolls," September 30, 2002; http://www.businessweek.com/magazine/ content/02_39/b3801011.htm.

Chapter 14:   Mara Der Hovanesian, "Charge!" August 9, 2004; http://www.businessweek.com/magazine/content/ 04_32/b3895001_mz001.htm.

TRENDS: Peter Engardio, "Business Prophet," January 23, 2006; http://www.businessweek.com/magazine/content/ 06_04/b3968089.htm.

CONTRIBUTORS

TOM LOWRY is a senior writer for *BusinessWeek*, responsible for the magazine's media and entertainment coverage. Prior to this position, Mr. Lowry was media editor for the magazine. He has penned and/or edited six cover stories since 2004, including "Can MTV Stay Cool?," a profile of CEO Judy McGrath and her efforts to remake her company for a digital world: "ESPN, The Empire," an analysis of how the hottest brand in sports plans to stay on top of rivals, and "Rupert's World," one of the first articles to add up all the Aussie mogul's vast and growing powers. Another cover, "MegaMerger," was completed in one day after Comcast made a hostile bid for Disney. "Nascar" ran the same week as the Comcast story as a regional cover on Southern newsstands, making Lowry the only *BusinessWeek*-er ever to have two covers in one week. He also wrote "Yao!," a sports biz story on the Chinese basketball phenom.

Lowry, an alumnus of the University of Delaware, was a Knight-Bagehot Fellow in Business and Economics Journalism at the Columbia Graduate School of Journalism. A newspaper veteran, he also did stints at the *New York Daily News* and *USA Today*, among others, before coming to *BusinessWeek* in 1999.

AMY BARRETT is the Philadelphia Bureau Chief for BusinessWeek, a position she assumed in 1998.

Prior to that, Ms. Barrett was the Philadelphia correspondent, covering the pharmaceutical industry and regional business from New Jersey to Baltimore. She assumed this position in July 1997. Ms. Barrett joined *BusinessWeek* in 1992 as Los Angeles correspondent and in 1994 became the Washington D.C. correspondent. She was responsible for covering banking and corporate finance.

Ms. Barrett came to *BusinessWeek* from *Financial World* magazine, where she began as a writer and was later named bureau chief. Prior to that, she was a credit analyst for Thompson McKinnon.

Ms. Barrett holds a bachelor's degree in finance from the University of Pennsylvania Wharton School of Business.

RONALD GROVER is Los Angeles bureau manager for *BusinessWeek*, a position he assumed in 1987. He has written numerous cover stories, including "The Future of California" (April 30, 2001) and "Hollywood Heist" (July 14, 2003), as well as articles on Disney, Michael Ovitz, Steven Spielberg, and the media and entertainment industry. Mr. Grover is also the author of the 1991 book, *The Disney Touch* (2ed., McGraw-Hill, 1996).

Mr. Grover joined The McGraw-Hill Companies, the parent company of *BusinessWeek*, in 1975 as a reporter for McGraw-Hill energy newsletter in Washington, D.C. In 1979, be became energy correspondent for McGraw-Hill World News in Washington, D.C. From 1982 to 1986 he was *BusinessWeek*'s congressional correspondent, covering economic and political issues, including tax reform, fiscal policy, and trade legislation. He moved to *BusinessWeek*'s Los Angeles bureau in 1986 as a correspondent, covering entertainment, politics, and other business news, which he continues to cover in his present post. Prior to joining McGraw-Hill, Mr. Grover was a reporter for *The Washington Star*.

Mr. Grover holds a bachelor's degree in political science and a master's in business administration from George Washington University and a master's degree from the Columbia University Graduate School of Journalism.

ROBERT D. HOF is the San Mateo Bureau Chief at *BusinessWeek*, a position he assumed in 2002. Prior to this position, he was a senior correspondent in San Mateo, responsible for covering the semiconductor industry, telecommunications, and other technology beats. Since joining *BusinessWeek* in 1988, Mr. Hof has covered a wide range of beats, including technology, state politics, and retail and environmental issues.

Mr. Hof holds a bachelor's degree in journalism from San José State University.

PETER BURROWS is the department editor of *BusinessWeek*'s West Coast computer coverage. Based in San Mateo, he oversees the magazine's coverage of the hardware world, from PCs and handheld devices to mainframes and back-office storage gear. He also covers some of the key West Coast computer companies, including Cisco Systems, Apple, and Pixar Animation.

Mr. Burrows holds a bachelor's degree in political science from Colgate University and a master's in journalism from Columbia University Graduate School of Journalism.

ANDREW PARK formerly a correspondent in *BusinessWeek*'s Dallas bureau, covered the technology beat, including Dell, Compaq and Texas Instruments.

A graduate of the Georgetown University School of Foreign Service with a degree in international law and politics, he worked briefly as a litigation assistant at Sullivan & Cromwell in New York. He earned a master's in journalism at the University of North Carolina at Chapel Hill.

DEAN FOUST is the Atlanta bureau chief for *BusinessWeek*, a position he has held since 1998. In this role, he oversees the magazine's coverage of all news from the eight-state Southeast, including *BusinessWeek*'s coverage of such leading companies as Coca-Cola, Bank of America, and Wachovia.

Mr. Foust holds a bachelor's degree in journalism and political science from the University of North Carolina at Chapel Hill.

He received the 1998 Gerald Loeb Award for Distinguished Business and Financial Journalism with colleague Michael Mandel for their coverage of the economy. He was also a finalist for the 1995 Loeb Award with another colleague for coverage of the Federal Reserve.

ROBERT CROCKETT is the Chicago Deputy Bureau Manager for *BusinessWeek*, a position he assumed in 2006. He is responsible for covering telecommunications and technology, the Internet and e-commerce, and race and cultural issues in business. Previously, he was a Chicago correspondent for *BusinessWeek*.

Mr. Crockett holds a bachelor's degree in English from UCLA and a master's in journalism from the Columbia Graduate School of Journalism.

SPENCER E. ANTE is the Computer Department Editor for *BusinessWeek*. He is responsible for covering computer hardware, software, chips and services, with a focus on the tech industry's biggest company, IBM. Previously, Mr. Ante was Internet department editor.

Mr. Ante has been writing about technology and business for the last eight years. Before joining *BusinessWeek* in February 2000, he was a staff reporter covering the Internet for *TheStreet.com*. Prior to that, he was a contributing writer at *Wired News,* a columnist for *Business 2.0,* and a producer for the Netscape NetCenter.

A New York and New Jersey native, Mr. Ante received a bachelor's degree from the Kelley School of Business at Indiana University and master's degree in journalism from the University of California at Berkeley.

CLIFF EDWARDS is a correspondent in *BusinessWeek*'s San Mateo bureau, where he covers Intel, the semiconductor industry, handheld- and consumer-electronics companies.

Mr. Edwards received both his bachelor's and master's degrees from Northwestern University, where he was also an adjunct professor of journalism for seven years. He was a finalist in Chicago's Charlie Chamberlain awards for wire service coverage.

ANTHONY BIANCO is a national correspondent for *BusinessWeek*. Since joining *BusinessWeek* in 1980, he has held the positions of San Francisco correspondent, staff editor, department editor, associate editor, and senior writer for the magazine. Mr. Bianco covered Wall Street from 1982 to 1992 and has since written broadly about American business.

Mr. Bianco is the winner of several journalism awards, including the Amos Tuck Media Award, the New York Society of CPAs Excellence in Financial Writing Award, and the 1997 National Business Book Award (Canada). He holds a bachelor's degree in humanities from the University of Minnesota.

JOHN ROSSANT was *BusinessWeek*'s European regional editor.

Mr. Rossant holds a bachelor's degree in history from the University of Wisconsin and has attended the postgraduate CASA program at the American University in Cairo.

MICHAEL ARNDT is a senior correspondent in the *BusinessWeek* Chicago Bureau. He is responsible for covering airlines, basic manufacturing, health care, and commercial real estate.

In 2000, Mr. Arndt was nominated for the Peter Ligasor award from the Chicago Headline Club for a story on United Airlines. His "Management Lessons from the Bust" article made him a joint winner of the same award in 2001. During the same year, Mr. Arndt made an appearance on the ABC *Evening News with Peter Jennings*. A successful year in 2001 was followed by his appearance with the PBS CEO Exchange in 2002.

Mr. Arndt started his career in 1980 at the City News Bureau and is a graduate of the University of Wisconsin.

DAVID WELCH is the Detroit Bureau Chief for *BusinessWeek*, responsible for covering the automobile industry. Previously, he was a correspondent in the Detroit bureau.

He is a graduate of the University of Pittsburgh.

DAVID KILEY is a senior correspondent in *BusinessWeek's* Detroit bureau, responsible for coverage of autos and marketing. Previously, he was the marketing editor for *Businessweek*, a post he held since July 2004. Prior to this, he was Detroit Bureau Chief for *USA Today*, where he primarily covered the auto industry but also wrote articles about the large Muslim population in Michigan. Mr. Kiley has held editor and reporter posts at *Adweek*, *Brandweek* and CNN. He has also worked in the advertising industry, holding executive titles at Interpublic Group agency Lowe & Partners.

Mr. Kiley is the author of two books: *Getting The Bugs Out: The Rise, Fall and Comeback of Volkswagen in America* (John Wiley & Sons, 2001) and *Driven: Inside BMW, The Most Admired Car Company in the World* (John Wiley & Sons 2004). He won the Ken Purdy Award for Excellence in Automotive Industry Journalism in 2001 for *Getting The Bugs Out*. He was elected the 2005-2006 President of the International Motor Press Association.

Mr. Kiley received his bachelor's degree from Fordham University.

STANLEY HOLMES is a correspondent in *BusinessWeek's* Seattle Bureau, responsible for coverage of companies such as Boeing,

Starbucks, and Nike. He also reports on the aerospace and defense industries and contributes to *BusinessWeek*'s annual "Best Global Brands" special report.

Mr. Holmes earned a master's degree from Columbia University's Graduate School of Journalism and a bachelor's in English from Western Washington University.

CHRISTINE TIERNEY formerly a correspondent in the *BusinessWeek* Frankfurt Bureau covered the European auto industry.

She is an honors graduate of Georgetown University's Foreign Service School and received her master's degree in journalism from American University.

JOANN MULLER was Deputy Bureau Chief in the Detroit bureau of *BusinessWeek*, responsible for coverage of the auto industry and other major Michigan-based companies.

Ms. Muller received her bachelor's degree from the University of Rhode Island and her master's degree in journalism from Northwestern.

MARA DER HOVANESIAN is the Finance and Banking department editor at *BusinessWeek*.

Before joining *BusinessWeek* in May 2000, she covered the mutual fund and personal finance industries for Dow Jones & Co. and Knight-Ridder newspapers. Her work has appeared in the *Wall Street Journal* and other major metropolitan newspapers nationwide.

Ms. Der Hovanesian received her master's degree in economics from California State University in San Francisco in 1990. She won a first place award from the Associated Press for Business Writing in 1996 and a Scholarship to the Institute for Political Journalism for Georgetown University in 1986.

Take your
game to the
next level
with the
BusinessWeek
Power Plays
Series.

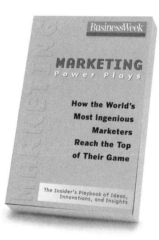

Visit businessweek.com/powerplays
Available everywhere books are sold.

Powerful Insight
for Powerful Players